BURIAL AND DEATH IN COLONIAL NORTH AMERICA

BURIAL AND DEATH IN COLONIAL NORTH AMERICA

Exploring Interment Practices and Landscapes in 17th-Century British Settlements

ROBYN S. LACY

United Kingdom – North America – Japan – India
Malaysia – China

Emerald Publishing Limited
Howard House, Wagon Lane, Bingley BD16 1WA, UK

First edition 2020

© 2020 Robyn S. Lacy. Published under exclusive licence by Emerald Publishing Limited.

Reprints and permissions service
Contact: permissions@emeraldinsight.com

No part of this book may be reproduced, stored in a retrieval system, transmitted in any form or by any means electronic, mechanical, photocopying, recording or otherwise without either the prior written permission of the publisher or a licence permitting restricted copying issued in the UK by The Copyright Licensing Agency and in the USA by The Copyright Clearance Center. Any opinions expressed in the chapters are those of the authors. Whilst Emerald makes every effort to ensure the quality and accuracy of its content, Emerald makes no representation implied or otherwise, as to the chapters' suitability and application and disclaims any warranties, express or implied, to their use.

British Library Cataloguing in Publication Data
A catalogue record for this book is available from the British Library

ISBN: 978-1-78973-046-3 (Print)
ISBN: 978-1-78973-043-2 (Online)
ISBN: 978-1-78973-045-6 (Epub)

Printed and bound by CPI Group (UK) Ltd, Croydon, CR0 4YY

ISOQAR certified Management System, awarded to Emerald for adherence to Environmental standard ISO 14001:2004.

Certificate Number 1985
ISO 14001

INVESTOR IN PEOPLE

CONTENTS

Acknowledgements   vii

1. Introduction   1
   Research Area and Background   3
   Literary Review   7
       Burial Landscapes   7
       Burial Grounds   11
       Grave Markers   14
       'Britishness' in Colonial Settlements   19
   Research Methods and Questions   21
   Terminology   22
   Chapter Summaries   28
   Conclusion   29

2. Effects of the Protestant Reformation on British Burial Traditions and British North America in the Early Seventeenth Century   31
   Pressures of Change – Burial Rites in Britain Preceding the Protestant Reformation   31
   Effects of the Protestant Reformation on British Burial Tradition   37
   British North America in the Early Seventeenth Century   43

3. Seventeenth-century Burial Practices and Landscapes on the East Coast   51
   Below the Surface   54
   Gravestones in the Seventeenth-century Atlantic World   59

Seventeenth-century Gravestone Iconography	65
Protective Marks in a Mortuary Context	68
Conclusions	76
4. Statistical Analysis of Seventeenth-Century Burial Landscapes in British North America	77
Settlement Organization in the Seventeenth Century	80
Statistical Analysis of Burial Ground Organization	95
Results of the Analysis	99
5. Case Study: The Colony of Avalon at Ferryland, Newfoundland	107
The British and Irish in Seventeenth Century Newfoundland	108
Evidence of Deaths at Ferryland	112
The Search for the Seventeenth Century Burials at Ferryland	114
Additional Case Study: Guilford, Connecticut	122
Guilford, Connecticut	123
6. Discussion and Conclusions	129
Discussion	129
Further Questions and Directions	134
Conclusions	138
References	*141*
Primary Sources	*141*
Secondary Sources	*143*
Index	*161*

ACKNOWLEDGEMENTS

I'd like to extend my thanks to a number of people who helped get this book together and to the presses! Thank you firstly to my publishers and assistant editors at Emerald for checking in and guiding me through the book-writing process and answering all the questions this first-time author had along the way. Thank you to my reviewers for sending comments and contributing to the final form of the manuscript. Thank you to Dr Barry Gaulton for his endless support of my research during my master's degree at Memorial University of Newfoundland, which ultimately turned into this manuscript.

A special thank you to Adam Montgomery, Lorraine Evans and my mom, Barbara Lacy, for reviewing and editing the chapters for me and for providing valuable insight. The largest thank you to my husband and partner, Ian Petty, for making sure I always had tea and for rooting for me. No book is a one-person job, and your support means everything!

1

INTRODUCTION

Archaeologists confront death on a regular basis. There is nothing abstract about this statement; it is merely a truth that comes in tandem with a profession that works with the dead and the landscapes, buildings and objects that were left behind. Sometimes archaeologists come face to face with individuals who died centuries ago, and that connection to the dead becomes much more direct. Archaeologists facilitate discussions of mortality, death and burial, whether it be through museum displays, writing, online discussion, lectures or tours of active archaeological sites. It is important for the field to engage with the topic, as a collective of professionals who can offer a platform for discussion with the public. It is valuable for our understanding of human history and of relationships within societies between the living and the dead to understand the death and burial practices of a group of people. Through this, we are able to construct a better picture both of a society's general and more specific relationships with mortality, how they felt about the bodies of their dead, interactions with funeral practices and how they dealt with the grieving process. An aspect of the funeral and burial practices in any community is where the dead are actually buried with relation to the living, what or which landscape is oriented for the dead as well as the living, within the community of the living. A little-known aspect of death and burial during the North American colonial period is the early seventeenth-century practices from the British Empire who founded settlements along the east coast of the continent. This is due to the lack of gravestones and often of written documentation to highlight those early uses of a space as a colonial burial ground. This book seeks to shed light on those spaces, how they were used and what they meant to their communities.

This book aims to achieve two primary goals: to look critically at seventeenth-century burial landscapes and their organization at North American settlements and to reflect on the settler relationship with mortality. Reflections of mortality and settlers' relationships with their dead are represented in the burial spaces they left behind in the seventeenth century, and in the organization of these spaces that were influenced by sociopolitical, religious and geographic factors. Turmoil in the British Isles between the beginning of the Protestant Revolution in the mid-sixteenth century through the English Civil War in the mid-seventeenth century shaped not only the religious and political landscape of much of the British Isles but also affected the burial landscape of colonial North America. Changes to funerary and burial practices from the early–mid sixteenth century were caused by disagreements between the Catholic Church and the newly ordained Protestant Church of England, whose attempts to remove aspects of medieval Christianity altered church practices and burial rites. The effects of the Reformation on burial practices in the British Isles will be discussed further in Chapter 2. Settlers who died in North America during the seventeenth century did not have the 'infrastructure' for burials found in the British Isles or the patterns of previous burials or structures to dictate where the dead could be buried, but they did have the influence of both old and new burial traditions to guide them.

This book will provide further understanding of the choices and elements that affected the development of the burial grounds and interments within the landscape of British colonial settlements in seventeenth-century eastern North America. While this period is widely studied by archaeologists, historians and genealogists alike, a large-scale study of death and dying in this period which explores aspects of the burial practices, organization and morbid spaces of colonial British settlements had yet to be compiled. The following chapters explore and clarify seventeenth-century burial practices in terms of funerals and burial practices, and burial ground organization by examining both the orientation of graves within these sites and the wider landscape of burial grounds within their associated settlements. Within these burial sites, gravestone-carving traditions as they developed will be explored, as well as folk traditions transferred from the British Isles west to North America.

The data collected during this project provides a unique spatial database for burial ground organization at a regional, coastal and international level. By comparing the results of the frequency analysis, these data provide evidence of trends in burial locations. This information can then be applied to understand the burial practices of newly installed settler communities and also aid in locating seventeenth-century burial grounds that exist in the historic record but of which no clear physical evidence remains.

RESEARCH AREA AND BACKGROUND

It is important to recognize that the settlements explored as part of this research were established on the traditional lands of numerous Indigenous groups in what is now the United

States and Canada. This includes the territory of Kecoughtan and Kiskiack in Virginia, Piscataway in Maryland, Tunxis, Sicoags, Wangunks, Quinnipiac, Wappinger, Paugussett, Hammonasset, Mohegan and Western Nehântick in Connecticut, Massechusett, Naumkeag, Wampanoag, Agawam and Wabanaki Confederacy in Massachusetts, Wampanoag in Rhode Island, Pennacook, Wabanaki Confederacy, Pentucket and Abenaki in New Hampshire, Wabanaki Confederacy, Aucocisco, Abenaki and Arosaguntacook in Maine and the traditional territory of the Beothuk and Mi'kmaq peoples on the east coast of the island of Newfoundland (Native Land, 2020). While historical documents often mention that the land was lawfully traded for, this was often not the case, and in the instance of sites like Jamestown, Virginia (Kelso, 2006), and Old Town Newbury (First Parish of Newbury, 2016), the settlers would face attacks for years, the results of imposing themselves on these lands. The author acknowledges the historical and ongoing atrocities to Indigenous peoples caused by colonialism in the United States of America and Canada. This research recognizes that historic settler burial grounds were established as the direct result of colonialism on these traditional territories and represent an imposed ownership of land by said settlers.

This research examined sites dating between 1607 and the 1690s, spanning the Atlantic coast from Virginia to Maine including the island of Newfoundland, and uses a case study of the remote, coastal settlement at Ferryland, Newfoundland. All 60 of the sites identified and studied were founded by people from the British Isles: English, Welsh, Irish and Scottish. Specifically, this study focused on settlements originally founded by British and Irish settlers during the seventeenth century. This does not include settlements that were originally founded by settlers from mainland Europe and later taken over by the British, i.e., New York City, originally Nieuw

Amsterdam (New Amsterdam), founded by the Dutch around 1609 and captured by the British in the 1660s. Dutch, French, Spanish and other settler nationalities were present on the continent throughout the early colonial period of the seventeenth century though are beyond the scope of this research. An expanded study of this nature which includes sites founded by these other nationalities besides British and Irish would benefit future research. Only sites founded by groups from the British Isles were included in this study due to the wide scope of their settlements as well as their similar political and social background to British settlement in Newfoundland. The author intends to conduct such a study in the future.

Newfoundland has long been considered a land rich in fish and timber and home to numerous bands of Indigenous peoples (Tuck, 1976). European exploration to the region first occurred around 1000 AD with the short-lived Norse settlement at L'Anse Aux Meadows. Permanent European settlement did not occur until 1610 with the founding of Cupids by John Guy under the sponsorship of the London & Bristol Company (otherwise known as the Newfoundland Company), followed shortly thereafter by Sir George Calvert at Ferryland (Cell, 1969, 1982). The background of settlement in Newfoundland will be discussed in Chapter 5, providing insight into the famously poor weather, high winds, long winters and rocky terrain, endured by those early settlers who arrived unprepared and unaware of their new environment.

Ferryland is the fourth oldest permanently occupied British settlement in North America and the second in Newfoundland. Founded in 1621 by Sir George Calvert, the First Lord Baltimore, Ferryland, is a National Historic Site of Canada and houses a massive collection of archaeological material in a museum near the site. Visitors can observe archaeological excavations each summer and see conservation taking place in the onsite lab. It is a unique site due to the early attempts at religious tolerance brought across the Atlantic by Calvert, and the use of stone as the primary building material when most settlements of the period were of wood construction, and the subsequent level of preservation due to this material choice.

Ferryland, also briefly known as the 'Colony of Avalon' by Calvert, was chosen as the main subject of this research due to the lack of identified seventeenth-century burials present at the site. Located on the southeast coast of the Avalon Peninsula, on the far east coast of the island of Newfoundland, the town is an hour's drive south of the capital city of St. John's and is still considered relatively remote. Buffeted by high winds and occasionally featured in the media when colossal icebergs drift by, the town has been shaped over the centuries by hard work and survival.[1] The 'Colony of Avalon' existed under several different governors throughout the seventeenth century, but despite reference to a burial site in the historical record, the location of said burials has not been identified.

This project was the first strategic attempt to find the burial site at Ferryland associated with the early occupational period (1620s) at the site. This was accomplished by investigating burial grounds and organizations in settlements of similar age, religious background, settler nationality and geographic placement to Ferryland, in doing so narrowing down the multitude of unexcavated areas at the site, to locations with a higher probability for burial ground location. These sites were then ground truthed, first through ground-penetrating radar survey, then followed by archaeological excavation in order to look for evidence of grave shafts in the subsurface. The results of these excavations will be discussed in detail in Chapter 5 of this book. Although the 1620s burial ground at Ferryland has not been identified at the time of writing, the fieldwork

---

1 The iceberg has been immortalized on Stéphane Huot's 2019 design for Canada Post's international stamps, for the 'From Far and Wide' series.

undertaken was the first comprehensive attempt to locate those early burials at the site, and the excavations expanded the understanding of the burial landscape as well as the site as a whole.

LITERARY REVIEW

Burial Landscapes

A burial as a space comprises the burial itself, the burial ground as a site and the burial landscape, i.e., the wider context of the so-called morbid space within its community. The creation of a burial landscape is influenced by the surrounding geography, social relationships with the dead, politics, religion, and personal preference of the individual's friends and family, as well as the deceased's own perimortem wishes. Many scholars have incorporated studies of burial grounds as sites, as the focus of their work as historians, archaeologists and anthropologists. The study of landscapes as an aspect of archaeology, and burial landscapes in particular, comes with the understanding that there is no set definition as to what 'landscape' is or what it should mean between one group of people to the next (Anschuetz, Wilshusen, & Scheick, 2001, p. 158). The burial landscapes discussed in this research encompass the physical spaces that house the graves, elements which make up the spaces that are not graves (e.g., Landscaping, decorations, tokens left on graves), the space's relationship with other aspects of the community and its living populations and activities, movements and emotions that were enacted within or associated with it. While the meaning of landscape indicates what one can see within the natural environment, a landscape should perhaps be thought of as the outcome of cultural interaction.

This separates the landscape from the environment (Bain, 2010). Ingold (1993) suggests that a landscape can only exist to those who have known and lived within that specific environment at any given point of time. Upon that reasoning, while we can explore the cultural impact of the burial landscape, we will never be able to experience or understand the space in the way that people in the seventeenth century did. This only leads to more questions about how a community, historically, would have experienced and interacted with their burial spaces. When considering the evolution of a burial landscape, a space which inspires certain behaviours and emotion from individuals, acknowledging these affects is useful in emphasizing the need to explore cultural background and individuality when examining land organization (Anschuetz et al., 2001).

Today, burial grounds and cemeteries are often viewed with fear, reverence for the historic dead or curiosity as a tangible link to a community's past. Yalom's *The American Resting Place* (2008) provides a look at the evolution of burial practices in the United States in two forms: a photo essay and summary of burial traditions cross major regions of the country. In her opening chapters, Yalom discusses the Native American burial practices and recognizes European settler impact on the communities who practiced them. Following this section, the discussion includes, but is not limited to, the gravestones of New England and discusses death in the South, burial grounds as real estate and landscape and the American west. Crucial to this book are the discussions of the burial ground as a property, as a feature within a community, and well as the history of 'marking the grave', which provide an overview on the topic as well as an excellent point of reference to refer interested parties to. Discussing the burial landscape as an aspect of the community allows us to consider how people in the seventeenth century may have interacted with their 'morbid' spaces and how these spaces affected them. This topic is particularly interesting when considering where burial grounds were placed within their communities, which reflects a group's relationship with death and burial, which will be explored later in this book.

Throughout the twentieth century and into the twenty-first century, research studies investigating the iconography and carvers of early colonial gravestones remain a popular aspect of historical archaeology, folklore and history for their connection to the past and its people. Research has also been conducted on burial landscapes in some regards (Worpole, 2003), a widescale study of burial landscapes in terms of settlement structure, organization and geographical comparisons has only briefly been the subject of study (Brooke, 1988), and this volume seeks to fill in some of the gaps in our base understanding of burial landscapes within the seventeenth-century British colonial period (Buckham, 2016).

Brooke's 1988 assessment of burial landscapes in seventeenth and eighteenth century Massachusetts provides the only statistical analysis for early colonial burial grounds within the study area. The conclusions drawn in his paper indicate that settlers moved away from more remote (i.e., not central) burial locations in the seventeenth century to central sites within their communities to the eighteenth century (Brooke, 1988, p. 465). Using statistical analysis of the relationship between the burial ground and the meeting house, gravestone styles within faiths and aspects of religious life such as baptism and marriage within three counties in Massachusetts, Brooke explores the 'collective ritual practice of a complex culture of death' (1988, p. 464). The statistics presented illustrate the arguments presented in text, indicating that in the counties examined in the study burial grounds were primarily separated from their associated meeting houses in the early–mid seventeenth century, with 83% of burial grounds separate from meeting houses in Middlesex County, 100% separate in Worcester County and 87% total in both counties (Brooke, 1988, p. 465). This sentiment shifted at the end of the seventeenth century and established burial grounds revised their priorities to match, constructing churches adjacent to previously separated burial grounds.

These data represent a base for which this book can compare Brooke's results to the conclusions gained during this statistical analysis, which revealed consistent results between Brooke's research and the data presented in this book. While Brooke examined the seventeenth century in passing and as a comparison for the eighteenth century, his primary study period, these data provide the only spatial information for burial grounds to their meeting houses in the area. It does not include other spatial features such as the centre of town, use of fortifications, etc., focussing instead on the relationship between the burial ground and meeting house (Brooke, 1988, p. 465). While this relationship is crucial, it represents only one of many factors we must consider when exploring early seventeenth-century burial ground development.

The article notes that early Puritan settlements, in the early–mid seventeenth century, illustrate a noted divide between meeting house and burial space, 'a marked segregation of the dead from the centre of civil and religious life' (Brooke, 1988, p. 466). This book will demonstrate that many burial spaces of Puritan origins examined in Massachusetts and Connecticut retain evidence of this divide but maintained their burial spaces within the centre of town, just not on the same property as the meeting house. The symbolic divide between funeral practices and the religious aspects of daily life is a manifestation of Protestant refusal to allow interference of 'a soul's final designation following death, such as prayer or burial in sacred soil' (Rugg, 2013b, p. 15). Burial grounds of this nature were municipally owned and were typically not consecrated grounds, as the Church of England did not explicitly require burial in consecrated spaces, and one could reach heaven without burial in a consecrated churchyard as a result (Rugg, 2013a, p. 15).

Burial Grounds

Burial grounds, both above and below ground, allow archaeologists the chance to study a contained demographic of people, 'which can deepen our knowledge and appreciation of numerous aspects of social history' (Tarlow, 2016, p. 6). Burial grounds inform on the living society's relationship with death, social position, gender roles, religion and the body in the same way that the physical attributes of each individual buried within them do (Tarlow, 2016, p. 7). Tarlow speaks to the archaeology of emotion when dealing with death and burial, noting that the emotional toll of studying monuments and the dead should not be dismissed from the research, and neither should the emotions felt by those who buried the individual(s) in question (1999, pp. 20–21). The idea that we as archaeologists or historians should not attempt to understand at least some aspect of the thoughts of those who we study would be to dismiss their humanity in association with the creation and use of material culture and by extension their burial landscape. This is not to say that historical thought can be fully recreated, nor can the experience of walking through a burial ground in 1650, or attending the funeral of a loved one in 1710 but that we should consider variables which would have affected how people were participating in this aspect of their lives. Tarlow (1999, p. 36) suggests that by examining material culture 'metaphors' and the way 'people's understanding of their world structures the way they relate to it', the emotive responses to objects, spaces and rituals might be better understood. By employing this theoretical approach to burial spaces, we strive to build a clearer image of what these spaces were like, how they were used and experiences and how they felt to exist within.

The contributions to the field of historic burial grounds began with the 'antiquarian' researchers in the nineteenth century during a period when attitudes towards burials and burial grounds were evolving within North America. The early twentieth century saw little change to these early studies (Mytum, 2004). While records beyond the gravestones themselves were uncommon, scientific interest in burials as an aspect of archaeology was increasing, as discussed by Harold Mytum (2004). Mytum's work brings up the idea that secularization of the colonial burial landscape through the creation of nondenominational public and private cemeteries through the nineteenth century meant that 'those who wished to emphasize a religious identity had to profess this through the memorial, rather than just the place of burial' (2004, pp. 138–139). Indication of religion through monuments was not a high priority in many early colonial burial grounds, but use of nondenominational and unconsecrated spaces in Puritan settlements and on the coast of Newfoundland may have been used as a reflection of religion much in the same way that gravestone iconography did to the different groups buried there.

Multiple studies have been undertaken on seventeenth-century burial practices in colonial North America, though unfortunately none have been conducted in Newfoundland, as no seventeenth-century British burials have been identified in the province at time of writing. Two studies in particular which contributed to the background research for this book were Riordan's work at the seventeenth-century burial ground at St. Mary's City, Maryland (2000, 2009), and Kelso's work on early burials at Jamestown (2006). Both of these settlements are significant to the research presented here, as they represent early initiatives by the British to colonize the east coast and have undergone widescale excavations of their organized burial spaces. Jamestown, the oldest permanent British settlement in North America, provided insight into burial practices guided not only by the requests of the Virginia Bay Company but also by availability of space. Kelso describes how the 1608 church was constructed in the centre of the fortified settlement made from sedge, earth and rafters, and that burials dug prior to the church construction were aligned with the walls of the settlement or with other structures (Kelso, 2006, p. 83). Work done at the site has uncovered not only the organization of the early burial landscape at Jamestown but also the coffins, grave depth, hardware and body positions of those buried within. Such information is crucial to understanding burial practices in the early seventeenth century and indicate what emerging traditions might have been developing there.

Riordan's 2009 published data from the 2000 report 'Dig a Grave both Wide and Deep', which details the burial practices at St. Mary's City, provide insight into one of the only large-scale excavations of a seventeenth-century burial ground. This settlement is particularly significant to this research as it was the second settlement founded by the Calvert family, with the land being granted to Sir George Calvert in the early 1630s after fleeing the harsh conditions of his colony at Ferryland, Newfoundland, then established a few years later by his second oldest son, Leonard Calvert. The settlement was founded under George Calvert's original principal, one of religious tolerance for all, a practice that did not exist in the British Isles at this time. Riordan's detailed research and study of the burial landscape, implementation of coffin shapes and nail orientation, body positioning and orientation of burials with relation to adjacent structures are the only details currently known of burial organization associated with the Calvert family in the seventeenth century. Along with providing valuable information for the case study, the studies conducted at St. Mary's City display extensive data of a community with mixed religions during a period when Catholics were persecuted in the British Isles.

Grave Markers

There has been a wealth of research conducted on the topics of gravestones and burial grounds, popularized initially by Harriette Forbes' 1927 book '*Gravestones of Early New England and the Men who Made Them*', which examined New England gravestones as both a piece of art and a historic document (reprint 1967). In the 1960s, Edwin Dethlefsen and James Deetz (1966) published their evaluation of New England gravestone art (reprinted in summary, Deetz, 1977), which used gravestone art as an example of how to use seriation charts in archaeology and discuss the changes in popular gravestone iconography through the seventeenth and eighteenth centuries. Harold Mytum's 2004 publication explores historic period burial grounds and monuments in the British Isles and North America. It is one of the only large-scale studies to cover the topic throughout the period, as well as across the wider Atlantic world. Mytum also discusses the use of monuments for commemoration in 'mortuary' material culture as a tool for recording the nature of death and emphasis on a 'good or bad' death (2017, p. 154).

Further research has been carried out by numerous academics including Debora Trask (1978), who focused on carvers and carvings in Nova Scotia and brought gravestone styles and trends to light in the Canadian Maritimes, an understudied area within the wider scheme of North

American colonial burial markers. Her research provides insight on iconography from the eighteenth century onwards in a region which traded heavily with the colony of Massachusetts, making it a significant contribution to the study of gravestone styles on the Atlantic seaboard. James A. Slater (1987), whose work identifying the colonial gravestone carvers of Eastern Connecticut is invaluable to anyone studying the region, broken into two sections, gravestone carvers and the burial grounds they worked in, provides insight into the distribution and range of styles visible in Connecticut around the turn of the century and continuing through the eighteenth century. Acting as a near-companion volume to Slater, James Blachowicz (2006) writes about the development and changes in gravestone carving in Eastern Massachusetts. While these volumes primarily investigate gravestones from the eighteenth and nineteenth centuries, they are significant as sources for the study of seventeenth-century burial grounds in that the sites very often predate the gravestones in question. While early seventeenth-century settlers may not have had the means or materials to erect elaborately carved gravestones, their presence within the landscape is no less significant. Studies that focus on later gravestones provide a comparison for earlier burial practices, as well as providing insight into the development of the sites themselves, which has been useful to this research.

Gravestone styles and burial practices are reflections of a society's relationship with mortality at the time of an individual's death. Gravestones convey information on the deceased, but the use of different styles of text, inscription formats and iconography can help identify their social standing, their occupation, their relationships and their views on mortality, religion and cultural identity (Haywood, 2019; Stanley-Blackwell & Linkletter, 2019). Academics have perhaps paid less attention to gravestones without iconography, and script styles, or graves marked with nothing at all. Some religious groups such as Quakers, and some early Puritans, did not approve of or even allow use of ornate grave markers to mark burials, but rather opted for simple unmarked field stones, wood crosses, plain inscribed stones or no marker at all (Brooke, 1988, p. 467; Ludwig, 1966; Stannard, 1977, p. 116). This was a result of ideas related to banning idolatry, or the worship of imagery, as part of the separation from the Catholic Church. While it is clear that not all Quakers and Puritans were so radical as to not have gravestones at all, many were, and this is a potential reason for the lack of early seventeenth–century gravestones. Eventually, the styles for who chose stone grave markers evolved as more and more settlers moved into the region from Europe, but the importance of uninscribed and biodegradable examples should not be overlooked.

A critical publication to the discussion of early colonial burial grounds in America is Baugher and Veit's 2014 book *'The Archaeology of American Cemeteries and Gravestones'* which discusses the development of burial grounds and cemeteries across the country through the archaeological lens. Significantly, they, along with Hopkins (2014), discuss an update from the strict 'death's head – cherub – willow' narrative, indicating that it was not a perfectly linear timeline. Indeed, examples of the death's head in use through the nineteenth century have been observed by the author in such New England centres as Salem and Boston. Baugher and Veit (2014) and Hopkins (2014) both discuss challenges with Deetz's hypothesis that the decline of the death's head was tied to the decline of Puritanism (1977, p. 96) They concur with historians Hall (1976) and Benes (1977) that the death's head or *memento mori* imagery of earlier colonial gravestones was not, in any affect, tied to Puritanism (Baugher & Veit, 2014, pp. 87–88). This was due to the popularity of the imagery appearing on gravestones long after the Great Awakening, which previously had been thought to have affected the use of the 'death's head' as peoples' ideas surrounding death 'softened', as well as the longtime appearance of memento mori symbols of gravestones of people who did not practice Puritanism such as the Jewish (Baugher & Veit, 2014, p. 89; Mytum, 2004, p. 171). Deetz and Dethlefsen's discussion of the Enlightenment and the Great Awakening of the eighteenth century is significant in that it reiterates the social, political and religious themes at play throughout the colonial period; however, it has since been demonstrated that the death's head and cherubs were implemented on gravestones of people from many different religious backgrounds and persevered beyond the 1730s–1740s, continuing to be a popular motif throughout the eighteenth century and even into the early nineteenth century in some examples. Gravestones sporting a death's head can be seen throughout New England, Atlantic Canada and the British Isles beyond the date ranges prescribed by Deetz, and outside of the Puritan/Calvinist faith, with examples appearing on Anglican graves in New York state, and Anglican or Catholic graves in Newfoundland, England and Ireland (Baugher & Veit, 2014, p. 89; Lacy, 2017b; Mytum, 2004, p. 171). These images were tied to a broader regional and cultural identity, rather than strictly a religious one. While there has been much interpretation into Protestant and Puritan use of these images to emphasize theology, it is also known that the Catholics used these same mortality symbols in a 'counterreformation ideology' (Mytum, 2017, p. 163). These arguments show the importance of revisiting and retesting research which is viewed as gospel in any field, using contemporary methods and new information to apply to old questions. Without doing this, the growth of knowledge stagnates.

The discussion goes beyond the stereotypical New England gravestone motifs and explores imported gravestones in Virginia, uninscribed markers and Moravian burial markers, demonstrating the reach of the field outside the confines of the upright gravestones of New England. While the studies attempted to utilize gravestone data as a reflection of demography, assuming a relationship between gravestone iconography and the population, this functionalist approach has since been disproven (Mytum, 2004, p. 7). The research presented in this volume, while focused primarily on the New England area, is bound by the temporal confines of the early seventeenth century, and future research on the topics discussed would expand the study to include communities beyond the white, British settler narrative.

As Sattenspiel and Stoops (2010, p. 8) discuss, the value of studying gravestones beyond the iconographic elements is represented in the demographic information they hold, which can often represent a study population more accurately than vital statistics, if those statistics turn out to be incomplete or inadequate. These data, including the name, birth and death dates, and other personal information inscribed on the stones provide insight that would otherwise be difficult to collect through the archaeological record alone. Part of gravestone and burial ground recording today is heavily focused on collecting this demographic information before gravestones are too eroded or exfoliated to be legible (Mytum, 2000). The potential for archaeologies of aboveground burial practices provides information which compliments and fills out the records otherwise only produced by the subsurface (Tarlow, 1999). The study of the gravestone, the burial space, the burial itself and wider funerary and burial traditions completes our understanding of practices at the time and what we can learn about the population who performed them.

'Britishness' in Colonial Settlements

In some cases, during the seventeenth and into the eighteenth centuries, burial grounds were located near the centre of their towns (Brooke, 1988, p. 465; Lacy, 2017a). In constant view, these sites were eventually closed and relocated or reopened outside of the boundaries of a town due to factors like overcrowding, growing health concerns and the concept that too much exposure to graves would cause viewers to become too 'familiar' with mortality (Dwight, 1823; Mather, 1713). Such sentiment was common in the nineteenth century and was expressed with eloquence by Dwight when he passed through the town of Guilford, Connecticut, remarking that 'it renders death and the grave such familiar objects to the eye, as to prevent them from awakening any serious regard' (Dwight, 1823).

Rugg (2013a, p. 18) discusses the theory of graveyards and cemeteries, remarking that the history of burial practices in England does not simply shift from churchyard to cemetery, and it should be understood that this binary shift did not exist in colonial North America either. As settlers came across the Atlantic, they carried with them their understanding of burial practices from their traditions at home, and these British burial traditions are reflected in the North American landscape, to a point. Traditions do guide though may not dictate all aspects of the burial culture which was developing in the seventeenth century, effectively creating a narrative between established churchyards, community burial spaces and a mixture of alternatives. As in England, the burial ground as an unconsecrated space existed outside of the typical choices of churchyard or the later developed cemetery model. As Protestantism did not require burial in consecrated ground, many Protestant settlers, specifically Puritans, embraced this ideal in the colonies. While retaining aspects of their 'Britishness' was important to the early settlers and many arrived in North America with the intent of one day returning east (Stannard, 1977, pp. 96–97), the colonial landscape evolved to reflect new traditions and practices. However, the Puritan distain for funeral ceremony in seventeenth-century England was mirrored in North America and residents of Boston such as Samuel Sewall grew concerned through the late seventeenth century at the increase of 'Common Prayer funerals' (Hopkins, 2014, p. 73). While they might still be utilizing some versions of British customs and traditions, the settlers on much of the east coast were growing separate from their homeland(s) by the end of the seventeenth century, with the memory of the Great Migration period far behind them (Hopkins, 2014, p. 73).

This trend away from 'Britishness' was slower in Newfoundland, where settlement was controlled for much of the island by the English government and paid for by economic schemes backed by companies or individuals of great wealth in the British Isles, such as Sir George Calvert and their identity still reflected British customs and ideals. While Calvert was trying to establish a settlement separate from the religious laws of England, the prejudices against Dissenters and Catholics were still all too present within the population at Ferryland. A Protestant priest denounced the practices upheld at the colony first, followed by David Kirke's own comments upon his arrival on the Southern Shore in 1638 (Kirke, 1639; Krugler, 2004, pp. 97–99; Lahey, 1998, pp. 29–31).

The backing of many early colonial expeditions to North America came from the desire for growing capitalist ventures by companies and individuals who were still tied directly to England, and the English Crown. A complex relationship was created in the early days of the seventeenth-century colonial period as a result; new settlements were being established under English custom and guidance but were also separate from it to a degree due to the geographic divide between the colonies and England. The Virginia Company was one of the first British economic business ventures in North America, most famous for financing Jamestown. The settlers at Jamestown were left with strict instructions on how to conduct their time and organize their settlement. It is clear in the archaeological record that the settlers' relationship with their church and burial space was similar to that of the stereotypical English town with a central church and burials within, indicating their strong ties to the homeland (Kelso, 2006, p. 50). While settlers' identities were often tied to their native countries, many settlers in North America also arrived to try and make a new life for themselves in a place that they perceived as 'uninhabited' or at least free for the taking.

RESEARCH METHODS AND QUESTIONS

This research comprised the collection of data for and building of a statistical frequency model and fieldwork to test the model's potential to guide excavations and inform burial ground placement trends in the seventeenth century. Data were acquired from literary history and geographical sources to determine the relationship between burial grounds and their associated settlements. The process included reference to historic maps, journals, accounts, and Google Earth Pro to compare descriptions and sketches of burial locations against the contemporary settlements. By utilizing the topographic features on Google Earth Pro, it was possible to assess remotely the elevation and slope of many historic cemeteries, a sample of which was ground truthed in order to ensure accuracy of data. This programme was used rather than LiDAR and GIS packages due to the cost and training required to access such data. The topographic data were a small part of the overall research objectives, and therefore the use of programmes beyond the accessible Google Earth Pro was not considered necessary. Data were ordered and analyzed using Microsoft Excel and SPSS (Statistical Package for the Social Sciences). Archaeological fieldwork guided by the statistical analysis results took place at Ferryland, Newfoundland, over a 10-week period split between 2016 and 2017. This text discusses the excavation and its results and conclusions.

The research asked whether there are noticeable trends in burial placements at the beginning of a settlement's establishment and if those trends could be documented within social or religious groups and regions. Sites for the analysis were chosen based on a number of specific criteria. Family burial grounds on private land were not included. The settlements were established by predominantly British immigrants on the Atlantic coast, and the location of their seventeenth-century organized burial spaces was already known. Special attention was given to settlements which had fortifications in order to determine if they influenced the placement of human graves. About 60 burial grounds were included in the study. In terms of geography, sites ranged from Hampton, Virginia, in the south to Trinity, Newfoundland, in the north (see Fig. 1.1).

TERMINOLOGY

Terminology applied to burial sites often differs between disciplines, regions and backgrounds, resulting in muddled terms and misunderstandings of usage on a regular basis. Due to the vague nature of a great deal of the language concerning burial sites, it is appropriate in this context to be more exact. This section will provide an explanation of the terms chosen to best represent the subject material throughout the research.

The term *burial landscape* will be used frequently. It refers not only to the burial ground itself but the landscape it encompasses, including soundscapes, views into and out of the site and interactions within the site. As an aspect of mortuary archaeology, the burial landscape includes both spaces

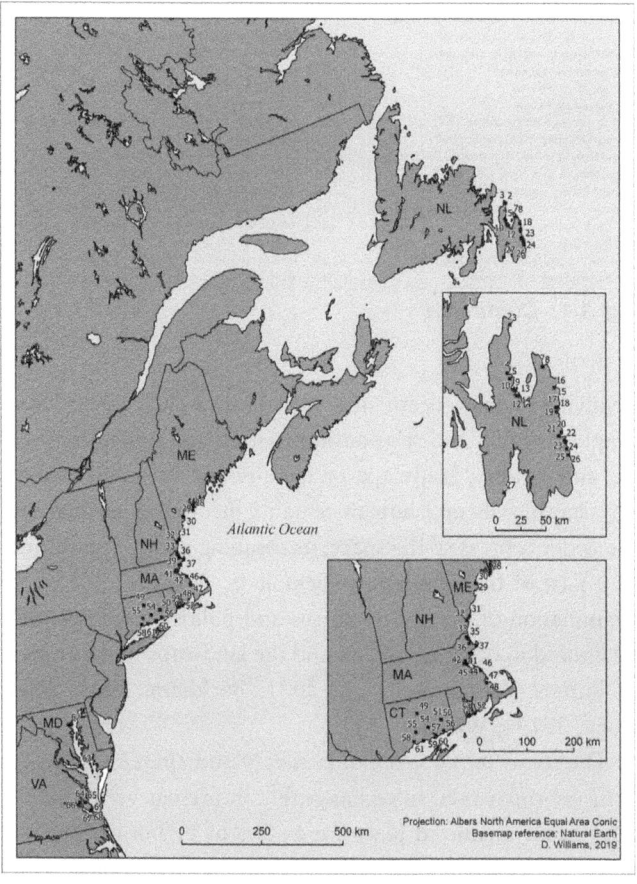

Source: Created by D. Williams (2019).

Fig. 1.1. Map of the Study Area.

Name	ID
St. Paul's Anglican Churchyard_>1729_Trinity	1
Old RC Cemetery_Front Road_Bay de Verde	2
Anglican Cemetery_Bay de Verde	3
Bethany UC Cemetery_Carbonear	4
St. Paul's_Churchyard_HarbourGrace	5
Old RC Cemetery_1799_HarbourGrace	6
Old St. Nicholas Anglican Cemetery_Torbay	7
Wareham's Lane Cemetery_Bay Roberts	8
Cupid's 1610+ Cemetery	9
Old UC/Anglican Cemetery_Brigus	10
Old RC Graveyard_PettyHarbour	11
Old Anglican Graveyard_Petty Harbour	12
Old Witless Bay Cemetery_1700's	13
BrigusSouth_Non-Denominational	14
Immaculate Conception Cemetery_Cape Broyle	15
North Side Burial Ground C18_Ferryland	16
Old Non-Demoninational Burial Ground, Ferryland	17
Old Cemetery - Port Kirwan	18
Old Cemetery - Renews	19
Old Graveyard_Branch	20
Fort St. George_Popham Colony_1607	21
Eastern Cemetery_1668_Portland_ME	22
Old Settler's Cemetery (Thrashers)_S.Portland_ME_1658	23
Old Burying Ground_York_1636_ME	24
Point of Graves_Portsmouth	25
Burying Ground of the First Settlers - Newbury	26
Old Town Cemetery - Newbury	27
Old North Burying Ground – Ipswich	28
First Parish Burial Ground-1644-Gloucester	29
The Burying Point_1637_Salem	30

Name	ID
Broad Street Cemetery_1655_Salem	31
Old Burial Hill 1638, MA	32
Bell Rock Cemetery, Malden, MA. pre-1649	33
Burying Place, 1635, Cambridge (Newtowne)	34
Copp's Hill Burial Ground - 1659	35
King's Chapel Burying Ground - 1630	36
Granary Burying Ground - 1660	37
Men of Kent Cemetery, 1624	38
Cole's Hill, 1620, Plymouth	39
Burial Hill, 1637, Plymouth	40
Ancient Burying Ground_1640_Hartford	41
Ancient Norwich Burying Ground_1661_Norwich	42
Norwichtown Burying Ground_1690s_Norwich	43
Little Compton Commons_1678	44
The Common Burial Ground-RI-1639	45
Old Cove Burying Ground_1690s_EastHaddam	46
Center Street Cemetery_Wallingford_1670	47
Ye Antientist Burial Ground_New London_1650s	48
Duck River Burying Ground_Old Lyme_1670s	49
New Haven Green, CT. 1638	50
Meeting House Hill Burying Ground_OldLyme_1660s	51
Cypress Cemetery - Old Saybrook	52
Guilford Green Burial Ground_1640s_Guilford	53
First St. Paul's Church_1692_BaltimoreMD	54
First Burying Grounds_1630S_St. Mary's City	55
Bruton Parish Churchyard_1678_Williamsburg	56
Historic Grace Churchyard_1691_Yorktown	57
Jamestown_VA_Churchyard_1607	58
Third Church_St.John's Episcopal_HamptonVA_1667	59
Second Church_St. John's Episcopal_HamptonVA	60

Fig. 1.1. *Continued*

involving human death and burial, as well as their topographic context and relationship to itself and other aspects of the surrounding landscape or community. Not only are the physical burials and human remains themselves studied, but the wider context of the space, its meaning and its significance as a part of the community (Semple & Williams, 2015). An examination of historical sources and political contexts must be utilized in order to understand the landscape in the context of burials (Anschuetz et al., 2001; Buckham, 2003, 2016; Rugg, 2013a; Worpole, 2003).

The terms *burial ground*, *cemetery* and *churchyard/graveyard* are often used interchangeably in present vernacular to refer to an organized place for bodies to be buried, but it is important to identify the differences of these types of sites and to use precise language, so the significance of a site's features and its origins are not lost (Rugg, 2000). Throughout the text, burial spaces of all kinds will be referred to as *burial grounds* as a general term. While 'burial ground' has a polarized meaning within Dissenter settlements, it can also indicate any type of burial space without denoting location within a community, connectedness to a church or indication of the denomination. *Burial ground* will be used as a catch-all, and when a Puritan site is being discussed, the specific meaning will be discussed.

The term *churchyard* or *graveyard* defines the area which surrounds a Christian church. This space is sometimes called 'God's Acre'; although in historic churches in the British Isles, the size of the churchyard often varies. St. Michael's, Lichfield, for example, covers seven acres (Rodwell, 2012, p. 296). Often enclosed by a wall, fence or in some cases roads or paths to border the space, consecrated ground is located within the space, in which the church has also been built as a place of worship. In places where churchyard overcrowding was acute, some parishes opened graveyards without a direct, physical connection to the church itself. This land was also consecrated (Rugg, 2013b). In these cases, the site could still be referred to as a *graveyard* but not a *churchyard* due to the physical dissociation from a church building. A *graveyard* typically holds members of the parish, and sometimes others who may have been buried there covertly, as occurred with some at the graveyard of the Protestant Cathedral of St. John the Baptist in St. John's, Newfoundland, as the result of Catholics avoiding a Protestant burial service (Pinsent, 1888).

Often, burial spaces are called *cemeteries* regardless of their type. This term is a catch-all in the colloquial language, but in fact, the term *cemetery* was not in use in North America during the seventeenth century and its use 'reflects a transformation of burial practices that first became common in the nineteenth century' (Baugher & Veit, 2014, p. 12). The term originates from the Greek word κοιμητήριον (*koimeterion*), meaning 'sleeping chamber', and references the idea of death as the eternal sleep (Baugher & Veit, 2014, p. 127; Sloane, 1991, p. 55). In academic discourse, a cemetery tends to have more specific meaning and denote a municipally owned, nondenominational, landscaped burial space with room between rows and graves, first referred to as a 'cemetery garden' or 'rural garden cemetery'. It only appeared as a term for a model of a burial site in North America during the first half of the nineteenth century, hallmarked by the construction of Mount Auburn Cemetery in 1831 in Cambridge, Massachusetts. With the opening of Mount Auburn, America saw the start of the 'rural cemetery movement' on the continent (Baugher & Veit, 2014, pp. 125–133; Curl, 2001, pp. 69–72; Linden-Ward, 1989, p. 293). The concept of the rural cemetery exemplified the style and 'romantic conventions of English landscape gardening' (Bender, 1988, p. 506), influenced by the opening of Père Lachaise Cemetery in Paris in 1804, generally regarded as the first landscaped cemetery (Baugher & Veit, 2014, p. 128). The changes in not only tradition but also in terminology shows a linguistic reflection of evolving burial practices associated with the colonial period, referencing the replacement of the disordered and 'unsanitary' burial grounds and graveyards with the preplanned and architecturally organized cemeteries (Baugher & Veit, 2014, p. 125). The natural beauty of sites like Mount Auburn created a public park, a space for relaxation and viewing the art of the monuments and a serene place for the dead to rest. In short, the evolution of garden cemeteries in mid-nineteenth–century North America reflects an evolving relationship and relation to death and dying itself.

In the way that *graveyard* indicated consecrated ground for religious burials, the term *burial/burying ground* was often used historically by settlers in New England and Dissenters in the British Isles to emphasis the unreligious ceremonial nature of the lots used for their burials (Hopkins, 2014, pp. 15–17). These spaces were primarily founded by Puritan settlers, but others such as the Quakers also employed the term to describe their burial sites as well. It defined an unconsecrated ground used for organized burial of settlers in the early seventeenth century. By refusing to bury in consecrated ground, and often refusing to even construct churches or have the grounds consecrated later, the settlers in New England in areas such as Massachusetts Bay and what is now Connecticut were staging a clear and obvious political and religious protest against the Church of England and the acting government at the time (Hopkins, 2014, pp. 9–10).

The terms *British Isles*, *British* and *Irish* will be used throughout this book to denote the places from where North American settlers and their descendants originated. Many of the settlements included here were financed by companies or individuals from England but comprised individuals from Wales and Scotland, as well as England. These settlers are referred to as *British* for the purposes of this work, and the settlements as *British-founded*. However, Irish settlers played a major role in the development and peopling of these colonial settlements and will be indicated separately. For the sake of a general term, the work will refer to settlers travelling to the Atlantic coastal settlements as coming from the *British Isles*. This is for simplicity, as the term covers England, Scotland, Wales and Northern Ireland as well as the Republic of Ireland. In using this term, there is no suggestion that people from Ireland are British.

The term *Anglican* was not in common use until the nineteenth century. To describe commonality in practice between Protestant Churches in the British Empire, this book will employ the terms *Protestant* when describing the Protestant Church practices. The term *Puritan* will be used to indicate the religious dissenter group characterized by radical reforms of the Protestant practices, made well known in North America by the early seventeenth-century settler emigration, as well as *Catholic*, for practicing Catholic settlers.

CHAPTER SUMMARIES

Several topics will be covered through this book, exploring influences on the organization of burial spaces in seventeenth-century colonial sites. The focus of Chapter 2 is to provide a background on the political and social elements of life in the British Isles in the years leading up to the Protestant Reformation and the resulting alterations to British burial practices that settlers brought to North America. While it is evident that the immediate effects of the Protestant Reformation had on burial practices were less dramatic than often indicated, changes were slowly being enacting and impressed upon the population.

Chapter 3 considers aspects of burial archaeology which tell a more detailed story beyond what can be seen on the surface. Through the examination of burial factors including gravestones, coffin structure and fixtures, burial position and personal objects such as burial clothing, it becomes possible to construct an image of not only the individual but also the society they lived in. This chapter also discusses the use of apotropaic marks as protection for the soul on gravestone. Apotropaic, or something which guards against evil or bad luck, is used to describe protective symbols which often appear in the form of graffiti on churches, homes and personal items (Champion, 2015).

Chapter 4 elaborates on the spatial analysis of burial organization and the concept of burial landscape. The chapter explores burial landscape organization within the 60 burial grounds included in the study. This study specifically examines the origins of burial grounds in early settler settlements, as they were originally laid out within the first iterations of their associated settlements. This widescale survey was examined through a statistical frequency analysis to explore commonalities between burial places and their settlement.

Chapter 5 discusses the results of this analysis as applied to the case study site of Ferryland, Newfoundland, founded in 1621, in order to inform excavations looking for evidence of the earliest seventeenth-century burial grounds. Ferryland is the fourth oldest permanently occupied British settlement in North America, located on the east coast of the Avalon Peninsula of Newfoundland, and was founded by Sir George Calvert, the First Lord Baltimore, whose family went on to find St. Mary's City and Baltimore City, Maryland. This project was the first attempt to locate the organized burial ground associated with Calvert's period of occupation at Ferryland, between 1621 and 1636. This chapter also explores a hypothetical case study, applying the same statistical data.

A spatial analysis of burial spaces within their settlements and against trends through the wider eastern seaboard can help inform ongoing and new research on seventeenth-century burial grounds, both known and yet to be uncovered. The results of the case study and its significance for understanding the variability of colonial burial practices is discussed in Chapter 6.

CONCLUSION

A burial ground is a fixture within all social landscapes, regardless of the form it takes within different cultures. Organized or not, individual burials or shared mausolea, a burial space is a reminder of generations past. Keeping the dead close and visiting their graves allows societies to maintain a connection with their friends and family. Settlers in the seventeenth century demonstrated their relationship with mortality and the dead through the organization of burial spaces. For settlers in North America, death meant dealing with a lack of 'the infrastructure found in the homeland' (Mytum, 2004, p. 43), which forced the community to adapt to the new environment. The trends in burial ground organization identified by this research inform on potential locations for a 'lost' burial ground dating to the seventeenth century. The study demonstrates the value of this method and its applicability on a regional scale. The data presented are more robust when applied at a regional scale and thus result in fewer variables when applying a statistical analysis of their organization. Through an exploration of burial organization, a dialogue may be opened about burial landscape evolution and the way in which relationships with mortality can impact burial organization.

2

EFFECTS OF THE PROTESTANT REFORMATION ON BRITISH BURIAL TRADITIONS AND BRITISH NORTH AMERICA IN THE EARLY SEVENTEENTH CENTURY

PRESSURES OF CHANGE – BURIAL RITES IN BRITAIN PRECEDING THE PROTESTANT REFORMATION

Society's relationship and interactions with burial are perpetually influx, with each generation changing traditions and introducing new ideas for dealing with mortality. In the twenty-first century, North America is transitioning away from embalming, which became popular in the mid-nineteenth century after the American Civil War, and casket burials towards more 'green' burial options, cremation and the advocacy of family funerals and care of the dead. While unlikely in North America even decades ago, in the sixteenth and seventeenth centuries, there was no embalming and personal involvement from families to care for their own dead was regular practice. People were used to seeing mortality firsthand, being with their families as someone died, and helping to prepare the body for burial within their own homes. An extensive discussion of the medieval burial landscape and how it may have imprinted traditions of landscape and use on settlers and the colonies is beyond the scope of this book, but social, religious and political shifts during the late-medieval to post-medieval period allow insight into the influences at play leading up to the seventeenth-century colonization of North America. Understanding that death and burial practices during this period, in the British Isles and into North America, are at the root of many of our contemporary practices is significant in the study of the archaeology of death and mourning (Powers & Renshaw, 2016, p. 160). With these influences came the development of an often-distinct colonial British burial landscape.

Prior and during the British colonial period, which began in North America in the early 1600s, Britain experienced political and religious upheaval following the Protestant Reformation, the Dissolution of the Monasteries and ultimately the English Civil War by the mid-seventeenth century. The Protestant Reformation occurred at different times throughout Europe and the British Isles, primarily in the sixteenth century. During the Reformation in the British Isles, which began around the early–mid sixteenth century (approximately 1529 with the separation from the Roman Catholic authority by King Henry VIII, though many other factors contributed to the unrest), many changes were made to the way in which people dealt with and understood death and the afterlife, although it would take decades for changes in belief to make their way into the majority of the British Isles. These events helped shape the British Isles, altering relationships with religion, politics and the way in which communities and churches handled burial rites. These impacts had a ripple effect, spreading to the way in which the settlers in North America created and organized their living spaces, and in turn their death spaces. Colonial burial grounds in the seventeenth century were ultimately shaped by the political and religious changes in Britain and Europe which lead up to and through the colonial period. In order to understand the ideas behind colonial burial sites, we must start by discussing the practices which preceded them in Europe.

Death and commemoration were at the centre of the late-medieval and post-medieval church in Britain (approximately the thirteenth century to the end of the seventeenth century, covering both these periods, though the post-medieval period extended beyond the seventeenth century). With relatively high mortality rates through this period, deaths of friends and family would have been a regular occurrence for much of the population. It is thought that in the late-medieval period in Europe, around 3 out of 10 babies would die during infancy (Thorton & Phillips, 2009, p. 1). In late-medieval Christianity (*i.e.*, medieval Catholicism), the dead retained agency through the universal promise of torment in purgatory, and thus gravestones and monuments were created to allow the dead to ask the living to say prayers to shorten the suffering and ease their stay (Marshall, 2002, p. 7). This was achieved through prayer and general thoughts of the deceased. Furthermore, all living and dead were connected through the 'communion of saints', or the spiritual unity between members of the Christian Church with Christ as the head. Purgatory is where the souls of those who still had temporal sins to repent at the time of their dead were forced to suffer, be purified and 'await with certainty the glory to come' (De Voragine, 1993, p. 282; Marshall, 2002, p. 11). The concept of purgatory became a driving factor and focus through the medieval period and became a central theme in peoples' daily lives. As a major focus of church doctrine and often of memorial practices as well, the mindset of easing passage from purgatory is reflected in both the fabric of the church and the churchyard, and both in the way that death and burial were approached, and how it was physically carried out. This was primarily accomplished through intersession, and chantry chapels, which were often constructed for that express purpose.

In order to die peacefully, one must obtain a 'good death' before the journey to purgatory, be it in concept or a physical place (Binski, 1996, p. 33; Curvers, 2010, p. 9; Houlbrooke, 1998, p. 183). To obtain a good death meant that the death was foreseen and prepared for, that the person was at peace, and surrounded by their family with your business concluded (Mytum, 2017, p. 155). An unexpected or violent death was considered a bad death, and potentially occurred due to interference from the devil (Curvers, 2010, p. 9). If the dying person achieved a good death, it would become important for their memory to be kept alive through prayer to lessen the time they had to spend in purgatory. This could be done through the construction of monuments asking viewers to pray for their souls and holding special masses on the anniversary of the death in order to speak of them with the congregation (Fossier, 2010, p. 135; Harding, 2003).

Architecturally, the quintessential English Parish has a church with a fenced or walled graveyard surrounding the building. Through the medieval period, the church could often be found at the end of a fork in the main village road, a bridge at the other fork and a castle or manor house at the base of the 'Y'. Having the church and burial space as a part of the heart of the village was common, allowing for people to see the realities of mortality every day, and interact with it regularly when going to church, or simply passing by. The collective need for salvation and absolution was a powerful force and affected the placement of bodies both in the church and in the burial landscape. Prior to the Reformation, wealth and powerful people were buried as close to the altar as possible, as there was a want to be closest to the most sacred part of the church. This option was much more expensive than the churchyard. The closer someone was buried to the chancel and altar, the more prestigious the location, thus the closer to salvation. The placement of individuals in the church was a conscious display of families' connections with the clergy and the community (Harding, 1992, p. 119, 2003).

In the decades leading up to the Reformation period, commemorating the dead through monuments and carvings expressed the need for remembrance by the family, but also anyone who visited and viewed the grave; however, most monuments were still found within the churches themselves. The imagery changed throughout the years, but the message was the same: pray for the dead. It is unfortunate that many pre-Reformation monuments and gravestones were vandalized, destroyed or lost through the sixteenth and seventeenth centuries as a result of changing beliefs and ideals. While it is likely that some early monuments were made from biodegradable material such as wood crosses, contemporary illustrations of churchyards prior to the Reformation show few crosses and even fewer stone monuments outside the church, showing their scarcity overall (Mytum, 2004, 2017, p. 160). 'Very few interments [had] any permanent memorial during the seventeenth century' (Mytum, 2017, p. 160).

Within the churches, monuments could range from simple stone ledgers set into the floor or on the walls which stated the name and death date of the deceased, to mass produced monumental brasses which allowed for customizable text to fit the individual, to elaborate tombs and chapels to commemorate the wealthy in a community. These brasses were most commonly decorated with praying images of the dead, shrouded and decaying corpses, and phrases imploring prayer from the viewer to help guild the souls. Duffy (2005, p. 332) writes that brasses could be obtained for relatively cheap prices from the 1460s onwards, through regional workshops.

These hard-wearing objects were cheaper than stone or alabaster effigies and could be produced using general templates and in smaller sizes, leading to their rise in popularity in churches by the mid-fifteenth century, and often provide a glimpse of the doctrine of purgatory (Duffy, 2005, p. 332; Houlbrooke, 1998, p. 344; Monumental Brass Society, 1988). In order to request prayers for the dead, the brasses would often depict one or more persons with their hands in prayer, a coat of arms and literal inscriptions which asked the viewers for their thoughts and declared the needs of the dead. These images and requests were part of 'intersession', or prayers that were said in order to help the dead through purgatory. The brasses could show the figures of the dead as they were in life, but sometimes they would show shrouded individuals or decomposing bodies in order to invoke the compassion and pity for the deceased, a version of memento mori, calling for their prayer while considering one's own mortality (Litten, 1991, revised 2002, p. 60). These corpse designs can also be found in the form of effigies, called cadaver tombs.

Around the exterior of the church, the burial ground would have surrounded the church or have been located nearby if needed; however, these three-dimensional grave monuments were typically more ornate and reserved for high-standing, wealthy members of society, prior to the popularity of what is thought of as a typical 'gravestone' today. These gravestones included effigies of individuals such as bishops or noblemen with swords by their sides, cross slabs or vaulted ledges in a cross-shape with 'gables' as the sides of the crosses. Smaller gravestones likely existed in small quantities or other materials, but the volume of gravestones that pre-date the Reformation are scarce.

Through the sixteenth century, families were directly involved with the dead body of their loved one. They washed and prepared the body for the funeral and burial, dressing the person in their burial clothing, or shrouding them. There was no routine embalming between 1600 and 1900 CE, and cremation was not a permitted option by the church at this time, as the body was needed whole and intact for the resurrection (allowances were made for saints and royalty, who might be buried in multiple locations) (Cherryson, 2019, p. 38). Embalming was not common, and when it did occur on rare occasion before the twentieth century, some body parts, the viscera, removed and buried nearby (Cherryson, 2019, p. 39). It was stated that the 'operation [was] so seldom performed, that very few...even of our best surgeons, have arranged all the necessary processes of it in their own minds' (Baillie, 1812, p. 7; Cherryson, 2019, p. 40). Cremation had previously been used on the British Isles, but with the introduction of Christianity around the fifth century, it had been pushed out of popularity and would not return until the late 1800s. The church was very involved in the death and dying of its congregation; bells were tolled for the deceased, and a priest led the solemn funeral procession and said the last rites over the gravesite (Binski, 1996, pp. 33–37; Curvers, 2010, p. 10). Prayers for the person's soul to leave purgatory had to be said again and again on the anniversary of their death. As involved as the church was, all the rituals surrounding death and dying were about to undergo drastic transformation under the Protestant Reformation.

EFFECTS OF THE PROTESTANT REFORMATION ON BRITISH BURIAL TRADITION

The ideals of church reform spread through Europe from sixteenth-century Germany, protesting the beliefs and corrupt nature of the Roman Catholic Church (Hillerbrand, 1968). The Protestant Reformation in the British Isles, while championed in earlier years by several different individuals, is more famously known to have begun when King Henry VIII severed England from the Catholic Church in an act of state, with support from the anti-Roman sentiment was already brewing across the countryside (Gaimster & Gilchrist, 2003; Hillerbrand, 1968, p. xvii; Powicke, 1941, p. 1). Henry VIII passed an act in 1538 which required all parish churches in England to have their own copy of the English Bible, which had to be made available to be read by citizens. This was not previously possible, as the Bible was often printed in Latin and the clergy kept many aspects of the church services out of sight behind the rood screens. In short, the church held the power and people were not privy to interpretations of the Bible unless those interpretations came from the mouths of clergymen.

In 1536, the monastic communities were disbanded during the 'Dissolution of the Monasteries', so that the people and government might benefit from their wealth – as well as crush any political resistance the powerful communities might exert over the government (British Library Board, 2017). Through the reorganizing of religious groups and access to services came a radical shift in the way that death, dying and the afterlife were perceived and enacted by the member of the church. The fabric of the Christian Church in England had been altered and after Henry VIII died and his son, Edward VI, was crowned, further reforms to what is known today as the Anglican Church continued, and with them continued the physical alterations to churches and their decorations (Stannard, 1977, p. 106).

The removal of the concept of purgatory was one of the main targets of reform for the Anglican Church, as while the concept of purgatory was not a feature of the pre-Reformation Church's sermons, it was widely understood that all preparation before and after death would help hasten the soul's journey through it (Duffy, 2005, p. 338). While prayer and Masses would no longer help loved ones on their way through purgatory, the Anglican Church still taught that your actions and sins on earth had an effect on whether or not one would enter Heaven or be sent to Hell. Calvinist reformers went one step further, believing that one's fate in the afterlife was predetermined at birth, and nothing you did on earth during your life would change what that fate was. The Puritans, believers that the Reformation did not do *enough* to 'purify' the church, put these alterations to extremes in the colonial settlements. Following most of the doctrine of Calvinism, they believed that humanity was corrupted by the original sin, and that each person was a sinner who deserved damnation.

The removal of purgatory from accepted doctrine came with a slow suppression of the now-banned practice of intercession, although the Book of Common Prayer never forbids the practice specifically (Curvers, 2010, p. 17; Gittings, 1984, p. 42). In fact, a form of intersession was retained in the form of priests who spoke the last rites over a body in its grave. Other practices which brought attention to the dead were also discarded, for fear of the continued belief in purgatory, such as bellringing on a large scale to honour the dead, or long and extravagant funeral processions (although people would think of other reasons to hold these). Of course, many of these traditions were so ingrained in social practices that they were hard to put an end to, especially in more rural areas where church and state had less power.

Changes within Christianity meant changes to the fabric of the church: the rood screens were removed to make the ceremony more visible and accessible to the congregation, and the altar stripped and replaced with 'communion tables' – one would expect that the location of burials inside churches would alter because of these changes, but this is not the case. Harding (2003) expresses surprise in realizing how little the preferences and rituals surrounding the placement of the body within the church changed through the Reformation. With the Dissolution of the Monasteries, the burial of individuals within ecclesiastic communities ceased, but peoples' preferences for burial locations within churches themselves remained relatively the same; they wanted to be near the altar/communion table, and outside in the churchyard, as close to the church walls as possible (Harding, 2003). While the practice of being buried close to the altar is evident before and after the Reformation period, the social reasoning behind the placement was due to the removal of purgatory. Being close to the altar would no longer ensure your stay in purgatory would be shortened, but it would display your social standing to the community for years after your death.

Commemoration of the dead during the Reformation and into the seventeenth century was also greatly affected by the changes to the state religion. Of course, burial traditions are ever evolving and continued to change through the seventeenth century and beyond. Gravestones and other mortuary sculpture were not particularly common outdoors in organized burial grounds prior to the middle of the medieval period, with gravestones and monuments to individuals being overall rare prior to the thirteenth century (Houlbrooke, 1998, pp. 360–361; Mytum, 2017). In fact, few 'proper' gravestones – what is commonly thought of as a gravestone: upright, stone, headstone, marking the burial – have survived that date earlier than 1600 (Bartram, 1978, p. 1). Memorials to individuals or families and works of art within churches were often a target of the religious reformers, who sought to remove aspects of 'popery', or images relating to Catholicism, from their religious spaces. As the Word of God was meant to be worshipped in place of images and idols, sculptures, carvings and paintings of saints of other figures in the churches were the targets.

The vandalism of choice was iconoclasm or having the faces and heads of figures scratched or torn off. It is a ritualistic killing of the individuals depicted, and their beliefs, and during the reign of Queen Mary I, with Catholicism reinstated, evidence shows that the focus of iconoclastic attacks were focused on

Protestant imagery rather than Catholic (Graves, 2008, p. 37). In the case of the shining monumental brasses, the metal was easy to remove and was often completely torn out of stone ledgers, motivated by the banishment of intercessional practices (Duffy, 2005, pp. 494–495; Monumental Brass Society, 1988). In many, or even most cases, this was motived 'by financial green, thinly masked by religious fervor' (Hutchinson, 2003, p. 450). These monuments were sometimes sold to be reworked into Protestant memorial brasses, and the backs of some of these surviving pieces contain images that hint at their former Catholic lives.

Monumental brasses and other forms of memorials regularly bore inscriptions as well as images to represent the deceased. Prior to the Reformation, Catholic epitaphs often asked the viewer to pray for the souls of the departed, with lines such as 'Orate pro anima' or 'Of your charite pray for the soule' (Houlbrooke, 1998, p. 347). Once the reforms began to take effect, however, the inscriptions turned away from asking for prayer and towards text which emphasized the written work, mentioned the individual's life and family, their Christian values, and often just their names (Duffy, 2005, p. 332; Houlbrooke, 1998, p. 35; Norris, 1977). We can see gravestones that simply start 'Here lies the body of' or 'This Stone Was Erected By' (these would also typically be all capitalized), and mention a relation or perhaps only the person's name, age and date of death. Inscriptions would 'record not the desire for prayers but the Christian virtues of the deceased' (Duffy, 2005, p. 332). These alterations to inscription styles directly reflect the destruction of medieval Catholic beliefs, and an attempt to separate the worship of images from the Church. Additionally, by removing the images of the dead from their community, they were being cast into anonymity (Duffy, 2005, p. 494). Many monuments and other religious works of art were destroyed throughout this period, and into the seventeenth century as the official religion of England switched back and forth between Anglicanism and Catholicism. The defacing and removal of monuments became so common that in 1560, Elizabeth I declared that there would be no more destruction of grave markers and monuments for the continued honour of noble persons and public servants, as well as genealogical information (Houlbrooke, 1998, p. 348). As a result, the artwork on some grave markers that included angels survived in rural areas (Sanghra, 2012, p. 57).

The practice of being buried in consecrated ground was considered less important to some groups of reformers, who wished to distance aspects of their rituals from the Church even further. While previously the body of a parishioner would be buried in land that was usually both spiritually and geographically tied to the holy space of the church itself, particularly staunch reformers like the Puritans did not believe that this kind of sacred space was necessary for the disposal of one's earthy remains (Hopkins, 2014). This included consecrated grounds which were spiritually but not geographically tied to a physical church structure. Because afterlife was predetermined, what good was burial in the churchyard going to do? As a result of the ending intersessions for the soul, the placement of the body would not help in the afterlife either. If a person would not spiritually benefit from being close to the altar, Puritans believed that it would be best to do away with the practice all together, moving from church and graveyards to burying grounds, using the term burial/burying ground to reiterate the unreligious nature of their burial spaces (Hopkins, 2014, pp. 9–10, 15–17).

It is these changing ideas in burial space organization that would become one of the biggest influences on the burial landscape of colonial British settlements on the east coast of North America in the seventeenth century. Political and religious strife in the British Isles came at a time of colonialism in North America, culminating with the English Civil War in the mid-seventeenth century, and saw the removal of the royal family from power. As a result, the layout of early settlements founded by the British in North America often reflects the struggles going on back home.

BRITISH NORTH AMERICA IN THE EARLY SEVENTEENTH CENTURY

Throughout of the Reformation, and the subsequent reigns of Elizabeth I and James I, the Protestant faith governed much of the British Isles, which resulted in Catholic spaces and individuals being targeted for religious persecution. Religious views affected the way that early settlers enacted their relationship with burial grounds and landscapes. Settlers coming into New England in the seventeenth century brought ideals of change for themselves, their faiths and their people, travelling for personal reasons, because of religious exile, or for economic expansion. Many of the earliest colonies, such as Jamestown, Virginia and Cupids and Ferryland, Newfoundland, were established not on the inspirational tale of a community escaping persecution but for the economic gain of the British Empire.

Jamestown, backed by the Virginia Company, Cupids by the Newfoundland Company (also called the Bristol and London Company), Ferryland, financed by Sir. George Calvert for its early years, or even Boston, organized initially by the Massachusetts Bay Company, were all early capitalist ventures in North America which were funded directly by companies or individuals in the British Isles (Lahey, 1998; Virginia Company, 1606). In the push to gather resources and precious metals in North America, settlers brought their beliefs, politics and ideals for how their new life would be.

An example of those changing relationships can be found within the settlements of the Massachusetts Bay Company and the Virginia Company. One of the first British economic business ventures in North America, the Virginia Company is best-known for financing Jamestown. The settlers at this fortified settlement which began with lean-tos were left with strict instruction on how to conduct their time, and how to organize their settlement. Archaeological records show that the settlers had arranged their church in a fashion similar to that of the British Isles; the first church was constructed in the centre of the 'town' and burials took place within and adjacent to the church (Kelso, 2006, p. 50). Jamestown saw regular deaths which lead to anomalous burial practices, partially influenced by the direct order to keep their dead out of the sight of the Indigenous peoples in case 'they perceive that they are but common men' (Virginia Company, 1606). The settlers at Jamestown were Anglican, and held their religious ties to Britain and the traditional relationship between the church and the communal burial space in some respects; with the first purpose-built church taking the central location in the early settlement based on archaeological evidence (Kelso, 2006; NPS, 2015). This is the case for most of the region (today the state of Virginia) during the seventeenth century as settlements were established and the use of family plots gave way to organized burial grounds. Statistical analysis of Virginia burial landscapes comes to the same conclusions. This relationship of the church and burials is to be expected, due to the political and religious foundations on which the early Virginia settlements were based on. It is quite the contrast to what we see when considering areas like Massachusetts Bay, or even what we now call Connecticut.

It is well known that the Massachusetts Bay Company had strong ties to the Puritan movement and the Great Migration into North America, beginning with the establishing of the Plymouth plantation in 1620. The strict Protestants, known later as the 'Pilgrims', were English Puritans fleeing England's Anglican rule, first to the Netherlands and then to North

America. Just as Catholics were persecuted for their beliefs, dissenters were not granted rights to worship as nonconforming/non-Anglican Christians until the Glorious Revolution in 1688 and they were not allowed funerals in churchyards until the Burial Act of 1880 (Sayer, 2011, p. 117). Puritans were just one group of organized dissenters in seventeenth-century England, which included the well-known Quakers, and other groups such as the Diggers, Enthusiasts, Muggletonians and the Seekers.

As settlements in North America did not have to fit into an already-existent town, settlers seeking a new start were able to mould their new home based on their beliefs, rather than the space left for them. Puritans were particularly concerned with the use of church rituals on burial practices (and in some cases other life events, such as marriage). In an effort to remove 'popely' aspects of burial rituals, the burial grounds that were set up in many major centres of New England were municipally owned, accessed by all and devoid of a holy presence (Hopkins, 2014, p. 27). These are all key aspects of a cemetery, save for the last part, but burial grounds and cemeteries are very far removed. The burial landscape of New England was, in many instances, used as strategically as possible to rebut against the Anglican Church, and its continued organization and cultivation of burial grounds as holy spaces.

Governor John Winthrop's final resting place was marked by civil, not religious ceremony in 1649 as he was buried in the unconsecrated dirt of Boston's first municipal 'burying ground' (Hopkins, 2014, p. 15; Morton, 1669). No prayers were said by his graveside, nor was he buried near a church's altar, for there were none to be found in the city. He was honoured with an artillery salute that befitted his station and service to the city, but religion took no place in the service (Hopkins, 2014, p. 15; Stannard, 1977, p. 110). Today this site is known as King's Chapel Burying Ground, and in the seventeenth century, it was in the heart of the growing city, easily accessible, unbounded and often used for grazing cattle. However, it did not hold the same influence that a churchyard in England might have. Instead, consider the 1645 Boston Book of Possessions map, redrawn in 1881 by George Lamb, which barely depicts the burial ground. It is plotted out with only a dotted line to indicate the edge of the property, but is not labelled in any way, a reminder that the space was nonceremonial and not connected to the church. By the time the map was originally drawn, this space had existed on the Boston cityscape for 15 years, and yet was still only depicted as a literal lot amidst the city. Lamb's copy, held by the Norman B. Leventhal Map & Education Center at the Boston Public Library, does not completely reflect the seventeenth-century mindset, but as a copy of a map from that period, it would be a strange choice to negate to label the burial ground if it had been labelled thusly on the original map. Later maps of the city, such as those drawn in the nineteenth century, have labels on the burial grounds. This appears to have happened once the effects of Puritanism were pushed back by the Anglican Church.

In the late 1600s and into the 1800s, earlier burial grounds in New England were becoming reassociated with newly constructed churches, as part of the 'Anglican Domination of the New England Government' (Hopkins, 2014, p. 8). In 1686, the Anglican 'King's Chapel' was constructed atop a portion of the 1630s burial ground in Boston, much to the dismay and anger of many of the city's residents. Subsequently, the North Church was constructed adjacent to Copp's Hill Burying Ground in 1723, and the Park Street Church was erected beside the Granary in 1810. This reassociation with a religious building occurred across New England, with churches being constructed on or near many historic burial grounds to establish religious control over those spaces (Hopkins, 2014). Sometimes this took the form of a meeting house, a structure used by Puritans as a municipal space where town business could be taken care of, along with religious services, but in the early seventeenth century, meeting houses were often built on different land than the burial ground. Brooke (1988, p. 469) writes that in the late seventeenth century, the relocation of meeting houses may be linked to the adoption of extended baptism.

Commemoration of the dead also changed with the migration to North America, though like their British counterparts, there are not many surviving gravestones from the early period of the seventeenth century. However, this is due to the limited number of established Europeans settlements in North America in the early seventeenth century, and was not mass destruction and iconoclasm during the English Reformation, as it had been on the British Isles. Much of what remains in these early colonial burial grounds are represented by the gravestones from the mid–late seventeenth century and through the eighteenth century, displaying everything from death's heads, cherubs and portraits to trees, broken flowers and eventually more religious or 'softened' symbolic iconography such as the willow tree and urns.

As already discussed, the rise in popularity of Puritanism saw the removal of many funerary rites within their groups that had become engrained in British tradition. It has been said that around 1650, the funeral customs in North America began to diverge from those in Britain, with new customs and traditions (Stannard, 1977, pp. 109–117). The author would suggest that the divergence began the moment the British settlers began to create their settlements free from the previously existing European templates. By allowing the creation of settlements under the British Crown in North America that were allowed religious freedoms, these settlements were able to explore options for settlement planning, which includes the planning of where burials were laid out. These newfound freedoms were not strictly limited to the Puritan movement, of course, but to the lack of limitations based on previously existent settlements in the colonies. The establishment of folk traditions in different regions swayed the placement of burial grounds, rituals and commemoration practices across the northeast coast and on the island of Newfoundland, and we see these patterns in some of the earliest British settlements in North America.

The seventeenth-century burial was done within a day or two of the individual's departure, as without modern refrigeration or the aid of winter, there was nothing easily obtained to stop the natural process of decay beginning before they were tucked under the earth's surface. The deceased's family would house the body in their home, and friends and family would visit the corpse there before the procession began from the home directly to the burial ground. Civil ceremony was not without celebration, as was evident in Boston (Hopkins, 2014). If a person died in an Anglican or Catholic community, the body might be transported to the church prior to burial for a service, but if the deceased was from a Puritan or another dissenter community, the church would not have been involved at all. A funeral procession in a strict Protestant community could wind its way through the narrow streets, often taking a long route for dramatic display, but most often moved from the house to the burial ground without a stop for a service (Brooke, 1988, p. 468). A prayer was not uttered over the grave, and the dead were buried in silence. This is not to say that they had done away with the funeral, but rather had adapted the proceedings to be less church-oriented.

> *When any person departeth this life, let the dead body, upon the day of Buriall, be decently attended from the house to the place appointed for publique Buriall, and there immediately interred, without any Ceremony.*
> (A directory for the Publique Worship of God 1645, in Stannard, 1977, p. 101)

This had been the practice in England for some Anglicans as well, showing the relationship between divisions of Protestantism in the seventeenth century. The tolling of church bells, the Book of Common Prayer and other ceremonial aspects that were once part of Catholic funeral practices were forbidden (Hopkins, 2014; Stannard, 1977).

This is not to say that the serious nature of funerals in the seventeenth century was the work of Puritans only, but of the reforms from Catholicism to Protestantism. The funeral reforms in the seventeenth century were shared across many nonconformist groups in the British Isles and into North America, and the solemn, quiet burial services were lamented by many who missed the ceremony (Stannard, 1977, pp. 104–106). While it has been previously argued that these practices, or indeed the symbology on the gravestones in New England themselves, was directly tied to Puritanism (see Deetz, 1977), the thought of that would be to 'invoke a stereotypical Puritanism' (Hall, 1976 in Hopkins, 2014, p. 1). In short, these supposedly grim services and imagery we often associate with the Puritans of New England was more likely a factor of the period, the society and the political and religious waters.

The diaries of Dr Samuel Sewall mention the death of Governor Winthrop the Younger in 1676, but only mention that he was buried in the Old Burying Place (King's Chapel). The funeral services were not mentioned, as there was none to discuss. Sewall later wrote of the death of his tutor, Mr Graves, in 1697, where he again did not mention a procession of the burial itself, but afterwards a friend sat on a nearby tomb and ruminated on how 'he knew he would be next' (Sewall, 1697, p. 454). To say the settlers were serious about death would be an understatement, as passage into death and the afterlife was an important life event. While early Puritan burial grounds, along with other dissenter groups, did not condone the use of iconography on their gravestones (or sometimes even gravestones at all), the use of memento mori gained popularity for gravestones, inspiration drawn from the late-medieval use of memento mori which remained *en vogue* for not just Puritans but many different groups of Protestants (Brooke, 1988, p. 467). Memento Mori, or 'Remember Death' in Latin, were used on personal items, paintings, furniture and other objects to remind the viewer of the fleeting nature of life. Perhaps it was best explained by Puritan Minister Cotton Mather when he wrote 'Truly, When we see a *Coffin*, perhaps of out own Dimensions, it becomes us to be very *Serious*' (Mather, 1713).

3

SEVENTEENTH-CENTURY BURIAL PRACTICES AND LANDSCAPES ON THE EAST COAST

Burial grounds, burial technology and practices never ceased evolving as new ideas and traditions grew from the old. Even today, what is considered a traditional burial, consisting of an embalmed body in a casket, lowered into a vault, often cement lined to keep the surface from slumping, appeared on the burial scene within the last 100 years or so. In the seventeenth century, settlers did not have access to a modern embalming or a crematorium, nor would they have wanted one. It is through their burial traditions that archaeologists and historians can explore what was done to bury the dead during this period.

Archaeologically, investigations of burials often look beyond the gravestones themselves, into the ground and the physical human remains. Everything from the grave shafts to coffin construction methods and styles, tell a little more about the people who built them, what was popular at the time, where they were getting their materials, and occasionally, who made the coffins. Often, these investigations reveal something about the general population as well as the individual. Excavations in Foxtrap, Newfoundland, of a nineteenth-century settler burial ground in 2016–2017 revealed coffins that were primarily constructed in the traditional tapered pattern, but included dozens of nails per coffin, sometimes of varying sizes in a single section of the coffin (Grimes, Lear, Munkittrick, & Lacy, 2018). This informed archaeologists that the community had the means and timber supply to outfit every burial with an individual coffin, but that they were using seemingly any, and every, nail they could find in order to do it. This speaks to the resourcefulness of the people, and the remote nature of settler communities on the coast of Newfoundland from the seventeenth century onwards. Ferryland, the second oldest permanent British settlement in Newfoundland, built a forge quickly upon arrival on the Avalon Peninsula in order to manufacture tools and nails that would be difficult to replace with more from England if they ran short part way through building a house, or a coffin.

While the depth of the grave itself was variable throughout the historical period in North America (Riordan, 2000), the remains of the individuals buried within maintain a wealth of information about not only that person but also population statistics such as average height, causes of death and diet. If they are lucky to have good preservation conditions, sometimes even elements like outfits and tattoos survive, depending where in the world one is researching. Studying a burial ground's population tells us what people were experiencing in their life and what caused it to end. Sometimes studying the dead of catastrophe sites gives archaeologists a better understanding of elements like 'demography and disease ecology [of a population] … which is exactly like a living population', such as Dr Killgrove's work in Oplontis and Rome, Italy, have pointed out (Killgrove, 2018). Forensic investigation of human remains, in the past and present, can lead to answers on what a person endured throughout their life, their movements, diet and illnesses, and by studying human remains we can build a better picture of the people who inhabited those communities.

Every aspect of a burial ground has a story to tell through many different channels of research, and the burial landscape itself, encompassing every aspect of the burial ground and its practices, remains no exception to this. The study of burial landscapes has been investigated for decades through applications of landscape archaeology theory, and historical investigation (see Baugher & Veit, 2014; Francaviglia, 1971; Rugg, 2013a; Worpole, 2003, among others). While there are limited surviving examples of inscribed gravestones in the British Isles that predate the Reformation (Bartram, 1978, p. 1; Mytum, 2006; Thomson, 2009), the use of a marker or defined space for burials post-Reformation indicates a continuation of the importance of death preparation during an individual's life. This preparation was translated onto the colonial landscape and is reflected in how they organized and utilized burial spaces.

The burial ground is a deliberate creation of a liminal space, an area between recognized areas or concepts, as a space created to house the dead and be utilized by the living. The necrogeography of a burial ground continues to architecturally and spatially evolve, often separated from the living spaces of a community by walls, fences or hedges. In order to understand such a scripted, socially rich landscape, researchers must not only look at the physical placement of the burials themselves but also examine historical sources and political context, religious affiliations and tensions in the society that created it (Anschuetz, Wilshusen, & Scheick, 2001; Rugg, 2013a, p. 216). Ideas of what would be appropriate for such a space have continued to evolve throughout the centuries, from carefully articulated cemeteries such as Mount Auburn (Sachs, 2010), back to the tightly packed historic burial grounds of early seventeenth–century Boston, to the quintessential English rural churchyard.

The early seventeenth–century settlers in North America were constructing settlements on land which they considered to be empty: the preexisting templates from older British settlements were not present there, and therefore did not *physically* affect the construction of new colonial settlements. While Nonconformists in Great Britain were eventually awarded the freedom to worship in 1688 with the Act of Tolerance, it was still considered illegal for them to hold independent funerals in established parish churchyards (Houlbrooke, 1999; Sayer, 2011, pp. 115, 117). In North America, settlers were able to set out a relationship with their burial grounds that they had previously been unable to do, an allowance that would not be afforded in England until the 1832 Reform Act (Sayer, 2011, pp. 115–117). In the seventeenth century, the relationship between a burial ground, the extended landscape and the settlement can be examined as a near-singularity; a fixed point in the social makeup of a society. While the churchyard tends to dominate the image of a historic burial ground in the popular consciousness (Worpole, 2003, p. 63), this ideal drastically shifted in the early–mid seventeenth century in many colonial settlements, bringing with it a plethora of altered burial practices, traditions and ceremonies. The analysis of these landscapes and the elements which go into them provides a holistic view of the relationship with major elements of everyday life as it was for settlers in the seventeenth century.

BELOW THE SURFACE

The death of an individual and the subsequent funeral are the physical elements that contribute to the purpose of the burial ground, but what comprises the burial ground itself? There is most often a delineated space, surrounded by fences or left unbounded; sometimes a church, gravestones or wood markers on the surface, and below the ground grave shafts cut to different depths holding shrouded bodies and coffins. Aspects of the burials differ between individuals, and each body is prepared in a manner dictated by materials available, fashion of the day, economic ability and other elements.

Shrouds might have copper pins holding the fabric folds closed, the strap of fabric around the chin to hold the jaw closed, perhaps a piece of fabric over the face as well. Bodies in coffins are surrounded by wood, metal nails on all sides holding the coffin closed. Their hands, knees and ankles might be tied with loops of cloth to keep them from falling to the side in the coffin, or perhaps they were dressed in burial clothes, rather than a shroud. It was increasingly common to see people in the seventeenth century dressed in prepared burial clothes more and more frequently than a wound shroud, which is sometimes depicted on medieval monumental brasses as being tied up at the top of the head and the bottom of the feet. While shrouds in the late-medieval period were tightly fitted to the body, during the sixteenth to the seventeenth century the shroud was essentially a large sheet extending about 12 inches above and below the body to tie closed (Cherryson, 2019, p. 40) A winding sheet, shirt and cap were typical readymade burial clothes, and in the seventeenth century into the eighteenth century, open-back burial clothes often resembled sleepware (Cherryson, 2019, p. 47; Gittings, 1984, p. 112; Litten, 1992, p. 76; Riordan, 2009, p. 88). Evidence of copper pins and staining on some remains at Jamestown indicates that they were either wrapping the bodies in a shroud within the coffin or at the very least using a strip of cloth to close the mouth, secured in place with a pin (Kelso, 2006).

By the late seventeenth century, the use of a coffin had become ubiquitous with burial practices in England (Cherryson, 2019, p. 41; Riordan, 2009, p. 81). Prior to individual coffins in graves, bodies were often shrouded and carried to the grave in a 'communal' or 'parish coffin', used only for transportation and not burial, but by the seventeenth century coffins were common among all people except for perhaps the very poorest of the society. Based on excavations at sites like St. Mary's City, Maryland and Jamestown, Virginia, seventeenth-century settlers preferred to continue this tradition where possible (Kelso, 2006; Riordan, 2000, 2009). When excavation of a burial shaft is undertaken, every aspect of the shaft is documented in order to understand how it was dug, how the coffin was constructed and how the individual was laid out within their grave or coffin. At St. Mary's City, excavations of the Catholic burial ground showed evidence of coffins in 32 of the 47 excavated graves shafts, with coffins becoming more popular through the mid-seventeenth century (Riordan, 2009, p. 82). Riordan reports that perhaps coffin use was restricted to the wealthy for some time in St. Mary's City, but from the mid–late seventeenth century, coffin use became more universal, results which are replicated in nearby settlements such as Middle Plantation and Clifts Plantation (2009, p. 83).

In Jamestown, VA, excavations have revealed dozens of graves: from the famous four chancel burials within the church, to Captain Bartholomew Gosnold buried with his pike, to unmarked graves of the general population which provide insight into the daily lives, hardships and burial practices of people at the early settlement. While the settlers were eventually buried in alignment with the churches, early burials which predated the church construction were found to align with the walls of the settlement itself. Individuals who died early in the settlement's history appear to have been buried within the fort, and it is these burials which are aligned with interior walls, likely in an attempt by the settlers to hide the number of deaths from the Indigenous people, per their orders from the Virginia Company. The individual known as 'Percy' or JR102C was buried in a hexagonal coffin, indicated by the soil stain left around the body after the wood had decomposed (Kelso, 2006, p. 126). His burial likely took place after Jamestown had been settled for several years. While Kelso suggests that the inclusion of a complicated coffin means the individual was more affluent, coffins were becoming more and more common in the seventeenth century. Other evidence of coffins at the site revealed the use of gable-lid coffins made from yellow pine, and a gable-lid rectangular coffin with a narrow base (Kelso, 2006, pp. 139, 142). Evidence of coffins is obtained either from surviving examples where preservation worked in our favour, remnants of the wood in the process of decay, or stains in the soil itself where the decomposing wood had altered the chemical composition of the soil. The wood stains or fragments combined with surviving nails, or their stains, can help us reconstruct how the coffins themselves were constructed.

Nails are not always the favourite or most glamorous artefact in archaeology, often eliciting groans from a field crew when they rattle around in the screen. While they might not be visually exciting, they can help nail down the date range of a structure, and even help us understand how a coffin was constructed. In particularly acidic soils, or unfavourable conditions which cause wood to decompose quickly, the nails might be all that is left of a coffin. Based on their location in the sediment that is left, we can get an idea of the dimensions of the coffin, the construction technique and the style of the container itself. While great variety was demonstrated at the St. Mary's excavation including rectangular, hexagonal and anthropomorphic, hexagonal coffins increase in popularity through the late seventeenth century and into the eighteenth century (Riordan, 2009, pp. 83–84). Coffin styles and accessibility was a matter of funds and available materials, as some sites may not have had access to the same quality of wood as the settlers at St. Mary's or other sides with high volumes of coffins, or the time to craft shaped coffins to fit the trends.

A line of nails down the centre of where a coffin once was indicates that the coffin had a gabled lid with one join down the centre, while a cross of nails suggests a pyramidal lid with two seams, usually on a hexagonal coffin. The way in which nails are facing in situ can let us know if the end of the coffin was nailed on to the ends of the other boards or inserted into the frame of the coffin (Riordan, 2000, 2009).

Before a burial could take place, the grave shaft had to be dug. While today the phrase 'six-feet-under' rolls off our tongues when referring to a grave, the six-foot rules was in fact not a rule at all. With programs such as HBO's apply named 'Six Feet Under' and other popular media representations referencing this specific depth, it has become the norm to believe that this was the depth of graves, however, historically it was not the case. In fact, a shallow grave, approximately 3 feet below the surface, is ideal for the quick decomposition of corpses due to ideal air flow which leads to bacterial growth and decomp (Order of the Good Death, 2019). The only definitive rules for a colonial British burial was to 'dig a grave both wide and deep', and colonial burials are often between a few hundred centimetres and just over a metre below the seventeenth-century ground surface, with graves in the Chesapeake often more shallow than other colonial areas, ranging between 2 feet to less than 5 feet below surface (Riordan, 2000, pp. 2–18). It was suggested by Rodwell (1989, p. 166) that the shape of the grave shaft can reveal whether a coffin is present inside the grave shaft. This theory was tested at St. Mary's City during the excavations of the Chapel Field cemetery; however, the results of that survey were not as black and white as one would have thought, with several round-end graves, proposed as 'coffin-less burial', showing evidence of coffins, and square-ended 'coffin burial' grave shafts were found not to have coffins in them at all (Riordan, 1997, p. 35, 2000, pp. 2–18). While coffin use was increasing throughout the seventeenth century in England and in North America, ground-truthing is the only exact way to know whether an individual was buried in a coffin or not.

GRAVESTONES IN THE SEVENTEENTH-CENTURY ATLANTIC WORLD

'Here lies the body of...' These are often the first words on a historic gravestone, or at least some of the most iconic. Decorated with grinning skulls, wings, bones and other symbols of memento mori, the historic gravestones of the east coast are an integral part of the burial landscape. The earliest burial grounds of the colonial settlements, however, were not populated by these stones so much as they were by just the dead themselves. Because many early burial grounds in North America had ties to the Puritan ideology, particularly in the areas known today as Massachusetts, Rhode Island, and Connecticut, gravestones were uncommon prior to the mid-1600s (Stannard, 1977, pp. 116–117). Even in the British Isles, the stereotypical 'gravestone', an upright-standing piece of shaped and polished stone with an inscription to a single individual, is rare to see dated earlier than 1600 (Bartram, 1978, p. 1), not because they did not exist but because the survival rate for pre-Reformation gravestones was lower than post. Early colonial sites were more likely to have indicated grave sites with wood markers which decayed quickly, unshaped or perhaps rough shaped field stones, which could easily have crude inscriptions on them, or with no markers at all.

While carved and inscribed gravestones were not as common in seventeenth-century colonial settlements as they would be 100 years later, there are some early examples of inscribed gravestones in North America, which survived as part of the archaeological record. The oldest example of a British gravestone in

North America was found at Jamestown and used to mark one of the four graves in the 1617 church at the site. This ledger, a large, flat, rectangular stone which lays flat across the grave, appeared to have a carved depression for a brass monumental brass in the shape of a man in armour, suggesting the stone was carved to commemorate Governor Sir George Yeardley (Historic Jamestowne, 2018). He died in 1627 and was buried in the middle aisle of the 1617 church. The ledger is suspected of being first damaged in the seventeenth century based on a quote from his step-son Adam Thorowgood II ordering a ledger to have the crest of his step-father found on 'the broken tomb' (Historic Jamestowne, 2018). The impressive ledger was carved from Belgian black limestone (Historic Jamestowne, 2018), suggesting that the stone itself was ordered from Europe after the death of Yeardley, having been carved and inlayed overseas and sent on a ship to the colony, rather than having the blank stone and monumental brasses shipped separately. Leading up to this period, it was common practice in England to commemorate the grave of an important figure such as a governor with a larger monument, like a ledger. These large, inscribed or inlaid stones can be found both inside the church and in the churchyard, and the cost of obtaining a stone that large spoke to the wealth of the individual interred below. A ledger appearing at Jamestown in the early days of the settlement directly follows the English tradition at the time, displaying Yeardley's importance to everyone who saw it. However, it is unlikely that the stone was carved and assembled in Jamestown. The practice of shipping prepared gravestones from the British Isles to colonial settlements can be seen in Newfoundland most prominently in the eighteenth century, but the example at Jamestown is the earliest.

On the east coast of Newfoundland, 9 or 10 settlers died in the winter of 1628/29 at the settlement of Ferryland, just a few years after the settlement was founded in 1621. At least two of their graves were marked with shaped and inscribed slate gravestones carved at Ferryland, which were shattered into multiple pieces. The fragments were recovered in a mid-seventeenth–century context, with the largest fragment recovered from the bottom of the eastern defensive ditch, and the smaller two fragments found south of the brew and bakehouse, one of the earliest structures built at the settlement (Carter, Gaulton, & Tuck, 1998, pp. 57–58; Gaulton, 2006, p. 88; Lacy, Gaulton, & Stephen, 2018, p. 93). It is not clear why the stones were broken, but several theories exist including the potential for the gravestones to have been deliberately broken in an act of vandalism, under the rule of the second Governor of Ferryland Sir David Kirke, who despised the former residences' Catholicism. Based on the border and curvature visible on each of the fragments, it is speculated that the stones were both semicircular in shape at the top, with a thin carved border around the edge. While neither recovered stone had a complete inscription, the largest portion read:

H[ERE] / LYETH T[HE BODY OF]
NICKHOLOS [H?]
WHO DE PARTED
[THI]S LIFE T[HE]
…. [MA]RCH…

This could have been the gravestone of one 'Nicholas Hoskins', who was a gentleman in the early days of the settlement (Carter et al., 1998, pp. 57–58; Lacy et al., 2018, p. 97), although more of the gravestone would be required to make a definite connection. The two small gravestone fragments refit, and read only: 'TH[E]/…[E/F?]AS[T E]…/6 2' which also does not inform much about the individual it was carved for, although the '6 2' could be interpreted as a 1620s date (Lacy et al., 2018, p. 94). It had been suspected by archaeologists in Newfoundland for years that the gravestones had in fact been carved at the settlement in the 1620s. A combination of visual geologic comparison and nondestructive portable X-ray fluorescence (pXRF) was used to determine potential stone quarry locations near the settlement, and test samples collected at a potentially quarried outcrop against the gravestone fragments and slate roof tiles that had been manufactured at the site (Gaulton, 1997; Lacy et al., 2018). Results determined that the gravestones were made from the same slate as the roof tiles, likely sourced from the same geologic formation, making them the oldest known gravestones carved by British settlers in North America (Lacy et al., 2018).

The two surviving Ferryland gravestones are the only gravestones which have been recovered to date from the seventeenth-century settlement and offer archaeologists a brief glimpse into the death and burial practices during those early years on the east coast of the Avalon Peninsula. Indeed, no mention of burials at Ferryland appears during the entirety of the seventeenth century, and until the mid-eighteenth century no burial site is indicated on a map of the entire area. The theory of vandalism results from the animosity expressed by Sir David Kirke upon his appointment to the settlement as Governor, wherein he wrote in a letter to Archbishop Laud:

> *I shall only add this one particular observation, out of what hath happened in the country heretofore and what I hope shall follow hereafter, that the air of Newfoundland agrees perfectly well with all God's creatures except Jesuits [Roman Catholics] and Scismaticks [Puritans]. A great mortality amongst the former tribe so affrighted my Lord of Baltimore [Sir George Calvert, Lord Baltimore], that he utterly deserted the country. And of the other sect, we have heard so many frenzies from our next neighbouring plantation [Massachusetts Bay], the greatest his Majesty hath in America, that we hope our strict observance and use of the rites and service of the*

> *Church of England, as it is our chiefest safety, by the blessing of God, whose ordinance we are constantly persuaded it is.*
>
> (Kirke, 1639)

Kirke was a known royalist, supporting and drawing favour from King Charles I and the Anglican Church. As is demonstrated by his letter, Kirke was not fond of Catholics, as was the sentiment in England following the Reformation, and much of his actions in Ferryland were done in order to erase the impact of Calvert and his supposedly Catholic settlement. This was achieved by destroying, altering and building over many structures created in the first 16 years of the settlement, ultimately changing much of the organization and purpose of the buildings (i.e., Calvert's horse stables became the drinking hall), and it is reasonable to assume that removing the gravestones would have been part of this reorganization.

While the Jamestown ledger had a large monumental brass affixed to its surface at one point in history, the Ferryland gravestones along with many other early colonial gravestones were not decorated. In some cases, this was likely the reality of the location and many settlers did not have the luxury of a gravestone carver in their settlement, and in some cases, it was the result of religious ideas turning away from the Catholic ideologies of iconography. While some of the settlers at Ferryland were Catholic, the majority of them seems to be Anglican. Puritan and Quaker gravestones are often seen as quite plain, and Puritans actively rejected the use of symbology and images during the earlier days of the reforms. Graves were often left unmarked or marked with simple stones with no iconography. While most colonial burial grounds in New England are famous for their elaborately carved stones from the later seventeenth to eighteenth centuries, the earlier examples that survive in these sites have almost no iconography (Fig. 3.1). While Stannard

Source: Photo by author.

Fig. 3.1. Gravestone of William Paddy, 1658, King's Chapel Burial Ground, Boston, Massachusetts.

states that 'only by the mid-1650s did New England's cemeteries begin to be populated not only by bodies but also with carefully carved stones to indicate the sites of burials' (Stannard, 1977, p. 116). While this statement is true for some Puritan or Quaker sites, it would be difficult to assume that all early burial grounds in New England were completely devoid of markers until the mid-seventeenth century, as the examples from Jamestown and Ferryland support. It appears that New England's Puritans were not quite as intense as those in England however, and some iconography did appear associated with early burials, with Samuel Sewall commenting that he did not know the intent for a coffin with a cross on it, at a funeral he attended in the mid-seventeenth century (Stannard, 1977, p. 116). In short, the iconography was often nonexistent or austere, but religious symbols did appear from time to time.

Common shapes and styles for early preiconography gravestones came in the form of likely wood boards or crosses which are no longer present on the surface but may have left an impression in the subsurface for archaeologists to find 'field stones' or unshaped or partially shaped rocks with no inscription as a marker for the grave, and later inscribed stones with a rounded top or irregular shape with little to no imagery present. This austere trend did not stick however, and by the mid–late seventeenth century more settlers were arriving on the east coast, and gravestones that were covered in imagery began popping up.

The Jamestown and Ferryland gravestones are the earliest examples of carved gravestones for British settlers in North America that are known of today, with the Jamestown ledger as the oldest grave marker, and the Ferryland stones being the oldest carved in North America. While these are the earliest known British gravestones of the seventeenth century, they are by no means the only ones on the continent. The next sections will explore details common on colonial grave markers throughout the seventeenth century, as well as a pervasive image that crosses the boundaries between church, household and grave.

SEVENTEENTH-CENTURY GRAVESTONE ICONOGRAPHY

The early colonial settlements of North America were the beginning of many traditions which are considered synonymous with the east coast to this day. As the settlements became more established, the culture began to grow its own traditions of gravestone imagery and styles which deviated slightly from those in England, Scotland and Ireland, while still reflecting much of the same stylistic attributes and influences. The earliest surviving gravestones, from Ferryland and Jamestown, directly contrast one another; two stones presenting an austere face with only a simple border and no other room for decoration, while the Jamestown ledger is decorated with monumental brasses and imagery to represent the individual buried beneath. While the monumental brasses display the wealth and status of the individual, and reference the styles for monuments popular during the medieval period in England, the simple, plain gravestones at Ferryland show the more austere and simplistic nature of early stones carved in the colonies. It is likely that many early gravestones had no to minimal imagery due to the lack of established artisans in the communities as they were being established. While we know there were slate cutters at Ferryland, they were brought over from Wales to deal with slate for construction primarily, and thus may not have had the skills to create elegantly carved death's heads or other imagery (Gaulton & Miller, 2009, p. 112).

The most famous imagery associated with gravestones in the seventeenth century is the death's head, also known as the winged skull. The skull, a mortality symbol, likely represents the dead individual and serves and as a reminder that 'death ere long will come for you'. The wings could suggest ascending to heaven, or leaving the body, as the death's head is often seen as a secular image for its representation of the decay of the body. The skull itself is part of a suite of *memento mori* motifs popular through the medieval period, and while the death's head was made popular, or perhaps made more prominent, by its prolific use on gravestones in New England during the mid-seventeenth and early eighteenth centuries (and into Atlantic Canada in the eighteenth century as well), winged skulls are often found as a decoration for burial monuments inside churches in the United Kingdom. The death's head appears in many variations in New England, from the classic skull and wings to more stylized crosses between skull and human face, with hourglass. Examples of a style common in Massachusetts which was sold north along the coast to sites such as the Old

Burying Ground in Halifax, NS., and St. John's and Ferryland, NL, by the early eighteenth century.

In the late seventeenth century, a variation on the winged skull appeared on the gravestones in New England, with the face of a child or of the deceased on the gravestone flanked by wings on either side. Sometimes called a winged cherub or a 'soul effigy', this image is typically interpreted as the soul leaving the body and ascending to Heaven. There are many variations on this image along the east coast, typically surrounded by flowers, protective marks, hearts and other decoration, the cherub image became increasingly popular through the eighteenth century within the study area. Like the death's head, cherubs typically appear front and centre on the top of the gravestone, and while there is usually just the one per gravestone, there are examples of two cherubs at the top of the stone. In other instances, double or triple gravestones to several members of the same family often appear with several death's heads or cherubs, one over each individual's epitaph.

Other iconography that was popular during the latter half of the seventeenth century included floral designs, bones, hour glasses, fruit, hearts, faces and, in some cases, figures representing father time and death itself. These motifs were peppered across many different styles of gravestones, with the most popular being a stone with a rounded central dome or lunette, two smaller rounded corners or finials, a border which was often decorated, and a central area of the stone for the inscription. This became the common formula for setting up gravestones along the coast during this period. Unfortunately, this book does not have room to cover the gravestone carvers of the seventeenth century, but this topic does not go understudied and there are many resources at one's disposal if you wish to learn more (Blachowicz, 2006; Forbes, 1967; Ludwig, 1966; Slater, 1987; Trask, 1978, to name a few).

Protective Marks in a Mortuary Context

An image that sometimes appears on gravestones, either in small quantities or multiple examples on a single stone, are protective marks. Apotropaic marks, forms of protection to ward off evil or bad luck, come in many forms, with the most common being the hexfoil, also known as the hexafoil, daisy wheel or witch hex. Much of what we know about these ritual protective marks comes from scholars in the United Kingdom such as Timothy Easton and Matthew Champion, as well as many volunteers recording the marks in homes and churches across the British Isles (Hoggard, 2019, p. 75). Most commonly seen in churches, protective magic was once central to the pre-Reformation medieval church (Champion, 2015, pp. 25–26). These symbols were carved onto church walls, fonts and near baptismal windows as a means of protecting an individual, or multiple individuals, whether it be their physical body or their soul. Champion writes that the three most common designs were compass-drawn designs, most commonly the hexfoil or daisy wheel, the VV symbol, and the pentangle or pentagram, and are tangible remains of folk beliefs that persisted through the medieval period and beyond (2015, p. 27). The whorl or pinwheel design is also very common in many of the same contexts. Hoggard suggests, along with Easton, that the hexfoil is a 'solar related symbol which by the early modern period had taken on the additional le as a decoy or spirit trap', thus acting as a form of protection in that regard (Hoggard, 2019, p. 85).

A hexfoil (also called the hexafoil) is a six-pointed star or flower-like shape inside a circle, often connected through concentric arches to other hexfoils within the same carving or image, and can be found carved into stones from the Roman Empire, throughout the British Empire into the colonies of North America and Australia, as well as across Europe (Evans, 2011; Ludwig, 1966, pp. 272–273). The hexfoils, along with the whorl design, were used through the seventeenth century for personal and group protection and were utilized on gravestones both before and after the early seventeenth century. They can be found in a funerary context as far back as 1600 BCE (Hoggard, 2019, p. 75). Although there are not many surviving examples on early seventeenth–century gravestones in North America, we know they were being used for protection in this manner along the east coast during this time period and the lack of surviving examples is due to the lack of surviving gravestones from this period. However, it is clear that the hexfoil was still used throughout the period, with examples of the symbol carved into chests, house beams and barns through the seventeenth century (Hoggard, 2019, p. 83).

Romano–British gravestones reflect the use of these symbols, such as the gravestone of Gaius Saufeius, dated to the first century AD which describes the motif as rosettes, flowers with six petals each (British Museum, 2019). Multiple early-medieval cross slabs bearing hexfoils dating to around the thirteenth century or earlier have been identified at Bakewell Church, Derbyshire, and although they are no longer in situ, the hexfoils appear to take the place of the traditional cross atop a pole on these stones. An excellent example of hexfoils as the central motif on cross slabs comes from Maughold, on the Isle of Man, and is dated to the early-medieval period (Kermode, 1907). This example is often referred to as a six-sided cross, as suggested by the chi-rho symbol present on the same stone. Whether or not the hexfoil was placed on the cross slab as a means of a stylized cross or as a protective mark in place of the cross, it was clearly intended as more than just a flower-like motif.

Likely introduced to the British by the Romans, and conversely brought to North America by settlers, we see examples of protective marks being used by many different cultural groups. The Pennsylvania Dutch emblazoned their barns in America with such protective folk hexes, hexfoils can be seen on some gravestones in Săpânţa, Romania at the 'Merry Cemetery', and in Slavic traditions, the hexfoil was associated with the god Perun and referred to as a 'thunder mark', appearing carved on the crossbeams of homes to protect against misfortune (Areta, 2018). When found in churches, the hexfoil is seen as a symbol of spiritual protection, which might explain its extended use throughout the centuries.

Through the seventeenth and eighteenth centuries, protective marks become more common inside the home and on pieces of furniture or objects such as an eighteenth-century Irish sailor's trunk on display at The Rooms Provincial Museum of Newfoundland and Labrador, which has hidden hexfoils on the top corners of the interior lid. These markers were scratched into the wood and later painted over, leaving them barely visible to the naked eye and hint at changing ideals within a society or the owner's own family. Other objects such as headboards, chairs and musical instruments such as the cláirseach (harp) were built in 1734 by the Irish artist John Kelly (Museum of Fine Arts Boston, 2018). It is clear through examples found inside the home on personal items or openings to the home, similar to protecting openings to a church, that the belief in protective marks was still active, and in fact was quite a common occurrence (Easton, 1999).

At the same time, a late example of hexfoils can be seen on the gravestone of Elizabeth and Thomas Brothers dated to 1808 at the latest, in Port Kirwan, Newfoundland. The gravestone is likely Catholic due to the high population of Irish settlers in the area during the eighteenth and nineteenth centuries, the IHS with cross in the centre of the stone, and the inscription which opens with 'Erected by...' a style popular in Ireland. There are two small hexfoils carved in relief above the inscription. This stone is unique because it is carved from locally sourced slate, rather than having been imported as many gravestones were during the early nineteenth century in Newfoundland (Pocius, 1981). Outport communities were more likely to have needed to source their own gravestone due to costs and the remote nature of some communities. The locally carved gravestone shows that the use of hexfoils in a mortuary context was still in use in some small part, in Newfoundland as late as the early nineteenth century.

Meeson (2005, pp. 44–45) questioned whether some otherwise Christian symbols had been secularized by the seventeenth century or whether they were still being utilized out of habit. The author would propose that it is a combination of these reasons as well as a continued believe in the protection of the image, explaining why we continue to see hexfoils and other images resembling protective marks on gravestones throughout the seventeenth-century burial landscape of eastern North America. This is not to suggest, however, that protective marks are uniquely Christian symbols, as evidence of their use in ancient Rome suggests otherwise. Through the early seventeenth century, British and Irish settlers began to move to the new colonies in North America, taking their folk traditions with them and implanting them in new communities. Folk magic was prevalent throughout the early British North America, often presenting itself in the form of witch bottles containing objects such as pins, bones and sometimes urine (Becker, 2005; Manning, 2014), markings on and inside buildings (Baker, 2018; Yoder & Graves, 2000), furniture and sometimes also gravestones.

As Ludwig displayed in his 1966 publication, clear examples of hexfoils have been seen on gravestones as early as the Roman–British period and can be found on grave markers in seventeenth century in the British Isles and in North America. It appears through the frequency of the imagery on buildings and furniture that gravestones were not the original ideal place for the symbols, with them only really becoming frequent in the later seventeenth century in North America (or earlier examples do not survive with as high a frequency as we would like). The most common motifs related to apotropaic symbols are the hexfoil and the pinwheel or whorl. Versions of these two motifs evolved with the developing gravestone carving economy within the New England colonies.

While elements of magic or witchcraft are often viewed as 'feminine', Augé (2013, p. 188) argues that while magic was expressed by both men and women in different instances, activities like gravestone craving were carried out almost entirely by men, indicating that the protective marks placed on gravestones were carved by men. She writes that

> *...some of these practices reveal male concerns, while other may have been undertaken at the request of a woman to address their own fears, and still other manifestations may represent mutual worries.*
> (Augé, 2013, p. 188)

The settlers in New England and likely the entire Atlantic coast were employing folk magic in the form of protective marks not only to protect the souls of the living, their families and loved ones but also to protect the souls of the departed, and potentially their bodies as well. This was carried out through a deliberate placement of protective marks such as hexfoils on gravestones (Fig. 3.2).

Ludwig (1966, p. 271) speculates that the 'rosette' or hexfoil was transplanted [to New England] just before it faded out in England, recognizing sparse English examples of hexfoils on grave markers. He also recognized their persistent use on gravestones in North America and their relationship to whorls in placement and usage but offers speculation as to their significance as a protective mark. He gives an example of the geometric disk, or web pattern in the Pecker family

Source: Photos by author.

Fig. 3.2. Detail of Three Protective Marks on Gravestones on the East Coast. Whorl or Pinwheel (Left), Hexfoil (Centre) and a Web Pattern (Right).

gravestone dated to 1727, a more scarcely identified mark, as a potential indicator of a child's grave, suggesting a range of this symbol beyond the use by one carver discussed below (1966, p. 226).

Due to the small number of surviving gravestones prior to the mid-seventeenth century in North America, there are not many early examples of protective marks on gravestones from this period. However, this is due to the lack of survival of early gravestones, and not based on the lack of use of protective marks in the colonial communities. We know that the symbols were pervasive throughout early colonial culture, an easy way to protect your home and loved ones against witchcraft and evil. Examples such as the Lydia Broun stone (Copp's Hill Burying Ground, 1680) have no other iconography save for a whorl in the centre of the lunette. The John Coney stone (Granery Burying Ground, 1689) features a death's head, vines and grapes at the borders, and a hexfoil in each finial. Yet another Boston example, the Thomas Smith stone (King's Chapel Burial Ground, 1693) is ornately decorated with a death's head and foliage in the borders, with a central hexfoil below the skull. In this example, a small circle and central dot were carved into the middle of the hexfoil. The symbol is also referred to as a 'daisy wheel', referencing its shape which resembles an abstract flower, and some examples of hexfoils in North American examples show it with more 'flower like' attributes, as you move further into the eighteenth century.

Protective marks are seen in the work of many different gravestone carvers along the coast, but two specific carvers produced a large volume of pieces with hexfoils, whorls and a web pattern with the eight points, and resembles the occasional connection of points in a hexfoil. John Hartshorne, Obadiah Wheeler and his contemporary Benjamin Collins were carvers in Connecticut in the late seventeenth into the eighteenth centuries, and examples of their work throughout the region are excellent examples of the use of protective marks on gravestones. Many other artists also produced gravestones with protective marks, and the images are scattered throughout the Atlantic world. An example dated 1699 in New London, CT, likely carved by John Hartshorne with lettering by the local carver Joshua Hempstead is an early example of his work and features large whorls in either finial. While it is suspected that this stone was backdated when compared to other gravestones by Hartshorne in the burial ground, it has been proposed that his gravestone carvings can date as early at 1697 (Mytum, 2004, p. 181). Other gravestones that resemble Hartshorne's style are present at New London's 'Ye Antientist Burial Ground', with examples of the web pattern, date to 1676 and 1687, respectively, and could be backdated. It is important to remember that the relationship between the date of death and the date of erection of the gravestone can be offset significantly from one another, with stones backdated and typically not stating the date of erection, outside of some scattered examples (Powers & Renshaw, 2016, p. 160).

Alterations of the symbols could have been deliberate, in an effort to hide the protective magic in plain sight in a region where communities could be less than sympathetic to magic-users (Emerson Baker, personal communication via email,

2018), or it could be an alteration that came with the imagery fossilizing as a popular decorative motif in a society which was growing further disconnected from traditions of the British Isles. Images and symbols can be adapted, losing their original meaning and transforming into an otherwise abstract pattern. Today, we are all aware of the alteration of symbols to twist their meaning (e.g., swastika by the Third Reich, or Thor's Hammer by neo-Nazis) or the co-opting of imagery as a decoration without meaning (e.g., Navajo Nation patterns or dream catchers). It is possible that their prolonged use on gravestones was a combination of use for their meaning and use because of their simple and eye-catching designs but without trace of need to place protection on the grave itself. As was already discussed, protective marks used to be commonplace in the context of churches, homes and personal objects throughout the medieval period in the British Isles, and even earlier in other parts of the world.

As these symbols, meant as positive magic for protection, were carried into North America during the colonial period, they were applied to personal objects and parts of homes, in a combination with other protective (or harmful) folk magic practices. It is likely that, like many folk magic practices, the meaning behind the action of placing the mark on objects such as gravestones was lost, but people kept doing it into the 1800s because they enjoyed the imagery or knew there was a tradition to put that specific symbol on a gravestone, perhaps without knowing why. The use of protective marks on gravestones persevered in North America, arriving in the seventeenth century and making their presence known as part of not only the magic landscape within the colonies but as an integral part of the burial landscape as well. A hexfoil on a gravestone to protect the soul of the deceased might have stemmed in some communities out of the loss of intersession, or general desire to ease the passage to the afterlife whatever the individual's faith might have been. Regardless, the marks were deliberately placed and worked into the iconography of the gravestone to bare a clear message to the viewer.

CONCLUSIONS

For decades, the iconography and history of gravestones on the east coast has transfixed visitors to historic burial grounds, capturing their attention with wide-eyed skulls and smiling cherubs. The carvers who created these works of art are responsible for preserving the memory of not only the individuals commemorated on the gravestones themselves but of a societal view of death and dying at the time of carving. In the early–mid seventeenth century, settlers moved from no gravestones, wooden markers or simple gravestones to stones with skulls and other *memento mori* symbology to remind the viewers that 'death ere long will come for you'. This was an extension of their desire to live in the moment, and also often represented a fear of death in a time when infant mortality rates were much higher than we experience today in most North American communities.

4

STATISTICAL ANALYSIS OF SEVENTEENTH-CENTURY BURIAL LANDSCAPES IN BRITISH NORTH AMERICA

There are many ways to conduct an analysis of the landscape. You can walk through the space, gathering an understanding for how it exists now and try to understand how it would have existed then. You can do aerial photography, use satellite imagery or drone scans to get an idea of the land that only a bird or an aeronaut high in a balloon ever get to see. These techniques are often combined with analysis of the subsoil: the flora and fauna, the microtraces of plants extracted from soil samples, the layers of burned charcoal noting fire and proteins on tools used for butchering. Historic accounts, if they exist, are utilized for their descriptions of landscape, paintings and sketches by intrepid or wealthy people moving across the countryside, documenting what they wished and leaving a trace of this past space and experience through their words or pencil lines. All these techniques are employed by archaeologists, often in tandem, to understand past environments, settlements and spatial organization around the world. Statistical analysis is useful when exploring landscape organization when looking at multiple sites with multiple variables, but like any other means of analysis, it is best used in conjunction with several other means of gathering information.

The survey discussed in this chapter was created as a study on the organization of burial grounds within their associated settlements on the east coast of North America during the seventeenth century. The sites included were chosen based on a number of specific criteria, with the end goal of building a database of early colonial burial ground locations, and use those data to create a statistical model capable of examining the frequency of specific patterns of burial ground locations within regions, time frames, religious backgrounds and along the northeast coastline as a whole. The analysis was developed to explore how burial grounds were organized during the seventeenth century, in order to inform future investigations, archaeological or otherwise at historical settlement sites in North America which do not currently know the location of their earliest settler burial ground. The sites selected for this study were established predominantly by British and Irish immigrants on the Atlantic coast or with direct access to the coast by a major waterway, which had already identified their original settler burial ground dating to the seventeenth century, the first burial ground established in the earliest organization of the settlement. The study area is defined by territory along the east coast controlled primarily by the British government but is only a representative sample of these earliest settlements.

There are many variables which contribute to the differences this study has identified in burial ground organization between settlements and regions. These include the proximity of the burial ground to the church or meeting house, the settlement itself being surrounded by fortifications or not and whether the landform that the burial ground is placed on was sloped or not. Individuals' burial practices during the seventeenth century were typically influenced by their spiritual beliefs. Catholic funeral and burial practices differed from Anglican, who again had different practices from other factions of Protestantism such as Quaker, Lutheran, Puritan or Baptist. As it often does today, the person's belief system and the society they grew up in will, for the most part, play a role in how and where they are buried or otherwise disposed of. Today just under half of the dead in the United States are embalmed, while just a few years ago the rate for embalming was over 50% of the country. Meanwhile, the primarily Buddhist country of Nepal cremates over 90% of their dead, in accordance with their faith. In the United Kingdom, cremation rates were at 77.05% in 2017, due to the lower cost and reduced space for what are often deemed 'traditional' inhumations, a figure which has risen steadily since 1960 when only 34.7% of the nation's dead were cremated, as the Catholic Church had not yet accepted cremation (Urns for Ashes, 2018). While geography, elevation and location within a settlement and the wider landscape have an impact on the burial landscape, these factors often have more to do with the availability of land than overall choice of the community. However, in settlements with both hills and level planes, it appears that burial spaces are more consistently located on elevated hillslopes when compared to the rest of the settlement. Whether for drainage or because a hillslope is not an idea location for building a house or farming, low hills are a common place to find burial grounds, regardless of which seventeenth century community is responsible for conducting the burials.

Overall, the study consisted of 40 burial grounds surveyed on the mainland of North America, and additional 20 settlements surveyed on the island of Newfoundland. The sites selected were founded by British settlers and predominately financed by British backers, whether they were the Virginia

Company, the Massachusetts Bay Company, the London and Bristol Company, and the Plymouth Company or private backers like Sir George Calvert or Sir William Vaughan. Britain was interested in colonization in North America for several reasons: economic gain, claiming the continent for the British Empire ahead of other European powers and for a few people, the escape from religious percussion. Settlements in North America during the seventeenth century represent a time when settlement building did not have to follow the pattern or available spaces left by previous settlements: the British considered this open and untamed wilderness, despite the obvious presence of the continent's native peoples. These settlements represent a new development in landscape and settlement interaction and the interaction between spaces of life and death during this period.

SETTLEMENT ORGANIZATION IN THE SEVENTEENTH CENTURY

The sites explored through this study extend from Hampton, Virginia, north to Trinity, Newfoundland. Sites in Newfoundland date definitively to the eighteenth century, but strong documentary evidence suggests that their settlements date to the seventeenth century, as permanent British occupation in Newfoundland began in 1610, with the founding of the Cupids Plantation, in Conception Bay. On the mainland of North America, 32 settlements were surveyed including 40 different burial grounds, all dating to the seventeenth century. While the main goal was to include the earlier burial ground in each settlement, it was important to include other earlier burial grounds and settlements, as they represent the formative years of that settlement, often undergoing several periods of resettlement and reorganization. Much of the research on these sites utilized historic texts, journals and letters, and unless archaeological excavation had been undertaken at the site such as St. Mary's City or Williamsburg, the information was gathered primarily from the histories of the settlements themselves, as well as any historic maps that were available. Never underestimate the importance of a sketch map. While this portion of the chapter will discuss a snapshot of the sites explored in the research, a complete list of sites that were included in the research can be found at the end of the section (Tables 4.1 and 4.2).

In the modern state of Virginia, sites used in this study were Hampton, Jamestown, Yorktown and Williamsburg from south to north, all settlements on the coast which were established fairly early in the development of this region, with the exception of Yorktown, which was not established until 1691. Settlements in the region we now know as Virginia (in the seventeenth century, the entire coastline was sometimes referred to as 'Virginia' by the British) show influences of the Anglican Church and keep with the model of the traditional Parish churchyard surrounded by, or directly associated with, burials. Jamestown is famously known as the earliest permanent British settlement in North America, founded in 1607, as the southern attempt to hold the northeast coast from the French, with the northern colony being Popham or Fort St. George. The first church in the fortified settlement was constructed in 1607 as one of the very first buildings, and shortly after it burned to the ground, and the second church was built in the centre of the fort by 1608 (Kelso, 2006, p. 24). While burials took place in several scattered locations during those early years in the Virginia colonies, organized burials also took place within and around the church itself. Most notable of these were the four chancel burials. For the formative years of Jamestown, the Virginia Company gave strict instructions to 'not advertise the killing of any of [the] men, that the

Table 4.1. Seventeenth Century British Settlements Surveyed, East Coast (40).

Site Name	Town	Date of Burial Ground Establishment
Men of Kent Cemetery	Scituate, MA	1624
Old Burial Hill	Marblehead, MA	1638
The Common Burial Ground	Newport, RI	1639
Cole's Hill	Plymouth, MA	1620
Burial Hill	Plymouth, MA	1622
First Parish Burial Ground	Gloucester, MA	1644
Jamestown	Jamestown, VA	1607
St. Mary's City	St. Mary's City, MD	1630s
King's Chapel Burying Ground	Boston, MA	1630
Copp's Hill	Boston, MA	1659
Granary Burying Ground	Boston, MA	1660
Ancient Burying Ground	Hartford, CT	1640
Center Street Cemetery	Wallingford, CT	1670
New Haven Green	New Haven, CT	1638
Burial Ground of the First Settlers	Old Town, Newbury, MA	1635
Old Town Cemetery	Old Town, Newbury, MA	1650–70
Old North Burying Ground	Ipswich, MA	1634
Old Burial Ground (Burying Place	Cambridge (Newtowne), MA	1635

Table 4.1. (Continued)

Site Name	Town	Date of Burial Ground Establishment
Bell Rock Cemetery/ Sandy Bank Cemetery	Malden, MA	Pre-1649
Bruton Parish Churchyard	Williamsburg, VA	1678
Point of Graves	Portsmouth, NH	1671
Historic Grace Churchyard	Yorktown, VA	1691
The Guilford Greene Burying Ground	Guilford, CT	1639/40
Little Compton Commons	Little Compton, RI	1678
Ye Antientist Burial Ground	New London, CT	1645–1652/1653
The Burying Point (Charter Street Cemetery)	Salem, MA	1637
Broad Street Cemetery	Salem, MA	1655
Old Cove Burying Green	East Haddam, CT	1691/1692
Duck River Burying Ground	Old Lyme, CT	1670s
Meeting House Hill Burying Ground	Old Lyme, CT	1660s
Ancient Norwich Burying Ground (Post and Gager Cemetery)	Norwich, CT	1661
Norwichtown Burying Ground	Norwich, CT	1690s

Table 4.1. (*Continued*)

Site Name	Town	Date of Burial Ground Establishment
The Chapell	Popham Colony, ME	1607
Cypress Cemetery	Old Saybrook (Saybrook Fort), CT	1635
The Old Burying Ground	York, ME	1636
Eastern Cemetery	Portland, ME	1668
Old Settler's Cemetery (Thrashers Cemetery)	South Portland, ME	1658
Second Church, St. John's Episcopal	Hampton, VA	1623/1624
Third Church, St. John's Episcopal	Hampton, VA	1667
First St. Paul's Churchyard	Baltimore, MD	1692

Table 4.2. Seventeenth to Eighteenth Century British Settlements, Newfoundland (20).

Site Name	Town	Date of Burial Ground Establishment
Old Non-Denominational Cemetery	Ferryland, NL	Unknown, potentially late C17th–18th
North Side/Anglican Cemetery	Ferryland	Mid-C18th
Cupids	Cupids, NL	1610

Table 4.2. (*Continued*)

Site Name	Town	Date of Burial Ground Establishment
Immaculate Conception RC Cemetery	Brigus South	Likely late 1600s
Old RC Cemetery	Harbour Grace (Brisol's Hope)	1799
St. Paul's Churchyard Cemetery	Harbour Grace (Brisol's Hope)	Mid-C18th
Old Witless Bay Cemetery	Whittle's (Witless) Bay	Early 1700s, perhaps earlier
Old Cemetery	Port Kirwan	Late C17th–early C18th
Old Cemetery	Renews	Late C17th–early C18th
Old Anglican Graveyard	Petty Harbour	Late 1700s
Old Roman Catholic Graveyard	Petty Harbour	1700s
Old St. Nicholas Anglican Cemetery	Torbay	Pre-1674
Bethany United Church Cemetery	Carbonear	1795
Wareham's Lane Cemetery	Bay Roberts	Pre-1766
Old UC/Anglican Cemetery	Brigus	Late C18th
Immaculate Conception Cemetery	Cape Broyle	Late C18th–early C19th
The Old Graveyard	Branch	Late C18th–early C19th
Old RC Cemetery	Bay de Verde	Late C18th–early C19th
Anglican Cemetery	Bay de Verde	Late C18th–early C19th
St. Paul's Anglican Churchyard	Trinity	Early 1700s (or earlier)

country people may know it; if they perceive that they are but common men, and that with the loss of many of theirs they diminish any part of yours, they will make many adventures upon you' (Virginia Company, 1606). As with much of Virginia, the burials in Jamestown took place on level ground, rather than the elevated places favoured in many other regions, due to the low topography of the region.

South of Jamestown, Hampton, Virginia, was founded in 1610 and was preceded by the construction of Algernourne (or Algernon) Fort on Comfort Point. After a settler was killed, land was taken from the Kecoughtan people, and the settlement known first as Elizabeth City was constructed on the banks of Hampton creek. The several burial grounds associated with the settlement were all constructed iterations of the first church, St. John's Episcopal Church. The church had three locations in the colonial period, and burials were associated with all three iterations (however the location of the first church site and burials has yet to be ground-truthed). Much like the other sites examined in Virginia, the English churchyard model held strong in Hampton. This 'model' suggests a church and churchyard organization which was popular for many communities in the British Isles, prior to the need for burial sites outside of communities and/or away from religious structures.

Family plots of private land were quite popular in Virginia during the seventeenth century, due to the spread out nature of the settlements themselves (Colonial Williamsburg Foundation, 2017). Family plots were beyond the scope of this project, and instead, the early community burial grounds were examined. Williamsburg established a community burial space not at its founding in 1633 but in 1674 with the construction of the Bruton Parish Church. Much later the settlement of Yorktown, preceded by the York-Hampton Parish, had a series of church-and-graveyard sets before the construction of a new church in 1691 in the town's present location with burials surrounded it.

The state we know today as Maryland was not as desirable as Virginia to the English in the early seventeenth century Sir. George Calvert wrote of his wish

> ...to remove myself with some 40 persons to your Majesty's Dominion of Virginia, where if you Majesty will please to grant me a precinct of land with such privileges as the King, your father, my gracious Master [in James I], was pleased to gaunt me here, I shall endeavor to the utmost of my power to deserve it.
> (Calvert 1629 in Cell, 1982)

Calvert wrote those words in 1629 after a difficult winter at his 'Colony of Avalon' in Newfoundland. He was ultimately granted permission to relocate to Virginia, but local pushback from Anglican settlers against having a Catholic noble and his group relocating in the region led to a land grant in the nearby region of Maryland instead. Unfortunately, Calvert would not live to see the new colony, St. Mary's City, as he died at Lincoln's Inn Fields in London in 1632 (Krugler, 2004, p. 118). His sons would go on to fulfil their father's goals of colonial enterprises and the creation of long-term settlements under his name.

Cecil Calvert inherited the grant for Maryland and endeavoured to uphold his father's wish for a settlement that operated with religious freedom (Krugler, 2004, p. 18). Founded in 1634, just two years after the First Lord Baltimore's death, burials at St. Mary's City took place outside of the fortified walls of the fledgling settlement, on a slightly elevated landform. The earliest recorded burials at the site date to the 1630s and surround a chapel which was destroyed prior to 1669 and was replaced with the 'Brick Chapel' (Riordan, 2009, pp. 1–3). While all the burials were oriented east–west, earlier burials were aligned more closely with the priest's house, then the early chapel, and later the Brick Chapel, suggesting the importance of the proximity to these structures as well as keeping in the Christian tradition of grave orientation (Riordan, 2000, pp. 3–4). A few decades after St. Mary's City, the settlement of Baltimore City was founded in 1660 on the banks of the Bush River and named for the Lords Baltimore to whom the land grant had been first given. The original location of Baltimore was slightly farther south than the present location, likely near the Aberdeen Proving Grounds, currently a military property. This location was identified through archaeological excavations which uncovered seventeenth century structures (Henry Miller, personal communication, April 27, 2016). While some accounts say that the bodies of the first church in this settlement near 'Pettite's old field' were relocated when the town moved north in 1765 (Beirne, 1967, p. 6), it is more likely that the church was relocated along with the city, but the bodies remained in situ. The location of this earliest church has not been identified, however.

Burials in Connecticut mark the move away from the Anglican/English churchyard model. The region was settled by many groups of people that identified as Puritan, fervent Protestant reformers who believed that the Anglican reforms in England did not do enough to separate the church from the papists or Catholics. Many settlements in this region, such as the famous nine-cell layout of New Haven, had a burial ground that combined aspects of communal space within the settlement and placed burials in the town green. Not many settlements in Connecticut were fortified, and burial grounds can be found in the centre of towns, as well as to the north or west of the core of the settlements themselves. A theme that can be seen throughout Connecticut and the Massachusetts area is that of Anglican reclamation of previously dissenter burial practices, through the physical placement of a church on a previously existing burial ground. This can be seen clearly at the Antient Burying Ground in Hartford, Connecticut, just north of the old town centre. Originally founded by Puritans, the first meeting house in Hartford was approximately 200 m southeast of the burial ground, suggesting a disconnect between the structure and the burial space. The first meeting house occupied this 'Meeting House Yard' from around 1636, but land for the burial plot was not delineated until 1640, deliberately separated from the meeting house space (Love, 1914, p. 11). After two meeting houses on the same property, the third and fourth meeting houses (with the fourth being the present-day church) being constructed on a large portion of the burial ground were not completed until 1807 (Center Church, ND).

The theme of dissociation from the earlier meaning of Puritan burial spaces and interaction with those spaces can be seen throughout many sites of this nature, as the ideals of Puritanism began to seem less appealing to settlers arriving towards the end of the seventeenth century (Brooke, 1988). New Haven, Connecticut, placed their burial ground in the centre of the town green, in the central cell of a nine-cell designed community established at the mouth of the Quinnipiac River in 1638. Once a central multipurpose space, today the majority of the gravestones have been removed and some in situ gravestones are housed within the crypt of the Centre Church on the Green, built on top of the site. The graves themselves, however, were not relocated, and the remains of early settlers are often unearthed when a tree falls and overturns the soil. This occurred when a 103-year-old tree fell as the result of Hurricane Sandy in 2012 (Winter, 2012). The trend of reducing the access or knowledge of colonial burial spaces through the eighteenth to nineteenth centuries seen throughout the east coast, with many sites bounded by walls or fences, having gravestones removed, or otherwise altering the way that visitors and locals could feasibly interact with the space.

The river-bound city of New London was established in 1637 but did not develop as a community until 1646 with the arrival of John Winthrop Jr. (Slater, 1987, p. 220). A plot of land on a hill was set aside in 1652 to 'bee for the Common Buriall place, and never be impropriated by any' (Blake, 1897, p. 37). While the meeting house was established nearby, it does not appear to have had a direct spatial connection to the burials, as dictated but the Puritan ideals of the founders.

The modern state of Rhode Island is famous for its city of Newport, another early seventeentn century settlement. Just north of the earliest planned streets, the Common Burial Ground was established in 1639/40. Like neighbouring settlements, the meeting house in Newport was not only not associated with the burials, but it was not built until 1699, on Fairwell Street where it still stands today (Bayles, 1888, p. 486). The town of Little Compton was also settled primarily by Puritans in the mid–late seventeenth century, and land was set aside for a common green in the centre of the settlement for the first meeting house, a common burial ground and a space for livestock to graze (Souza, 2016). However, unlike Guilford and New Haven, Connecticut, Little Compton Common remains filled with in gravestones, the way its founders intended it to be.

Massachusetts is famous for its history of early European settlers and associations with the Puritan colony. A large movement of Puritans (among others) flooded the area, thanks to the Massachusetts Bay Company and the Great Migration of the 1630s. Permanent British settlement in the area began with that of the Plymouth Colony whose settlers first came to the bay in 1620. Settlers at Plymouth established two burial grounds in the early 1620s; Cole's Hill, east of the settlement, was used first to bury the settlers who died in the first winter, and the second at Burial Hill was established in 1622 within the then-fortified settlement (Perkins, 1902, p. 9). However, unlike later Puritan settlements, Plymouth built their meeting house (and large defensive structure) adjacent to this burial ground (Perkins, 1902, p. 9).

The epitome of the 'Puritan' city is Boston, Massachusetts. Boston is known for such figures as Captain John Winthrop, who led the Winthrop Fleet in 1630, Puritan preachers Cotton and Instance Mather, and in the nineteenth century, the incomparable Isabella Stewart Gardner, founder of the 'Puritan on the outside, Italian flamboyance on the inside' Fenway Count, now known as the Isabella Stewart Gardner Museum. The city centre features three organized burial grounds within the limits of the seventeenth century settlement: the Common Burying Ground (known today as King's Chapel Burying Ground) opened in 1630, Copp's Hill to the north of the city centre opened in 1659 and the Granary Burying Ground in the city centre in 1660. These sites exhibit similar features such as elevated ground, all were treated as open land for burials, walking and openly engaging with the spaces and all three were overtaken by association with later-constructed Anglican churches. In the case of King's Chapel, the church was built directly on top of the site, displacing remains and gravestones. On the map of Old Boston from the 1645 Book of Possessions, redrawn in 1881 by George Lamb, the Common Burying Ground, which had been around for 15 years, was marked with only a dotted line marking the space with no labels at all. While this could have been an omission by the part of the nineteenth century artist, it would be an odd one, as other surviving maps of the city from this period clearly denote each burial site within the city. In choosing to leave the space unlabelled, it is a blasé reminder of the Puritan impression of the significance of a burial space with regard to spiritual well-being.

North of Boston, the town of Malden's Common Burying Ground was established to the west of the centre of town in

1649. It appears that they built a meeting house nearby, but it was not completed until 1660 and was not associated with the space directly, typical for the region as the town was mostly made up of Puritan immigrants, associated with the Great Migration (Corey, 1899, pp. 1633–1785). However, the nearby settlement of Marblehead which originated in the early 1630s as part of Salem, MA, was made up of predominantly Christian settlers who did not follow the Calvinist Church, as was typical of Puritanism (Goodwin, ND, p. 16). It is therefore not surprising to see that the first meeting house of Marblehead was erected at the same location chosen for the burial ground in 1638, the same year the burial ground opened for use (Roads, Jr, 1880, p. 14). Near the north edge of Massachusetts, the settlement of Newbury (Old Town) was established in 1635/8 approximately 6 km south of the present town of Newburyport. Its 'Burial Ground of the First Settlers' was established with the founding of the settlement to the north of town and is barely marked on the road today. The 'Old Meeting House' was built at an unknown date, approximately 450 m to the south (First Parish of Newbury, 2016; Moody, 1935).

Several settlements were also surveyed in the northern Atlantic states. In New Hampshire, the historic Point of Graves burial ground was designated in 1671 near Strawberry Bank, where the first settlers built their homes in the 1630s (Keene, Keene, & Auger, 1999; Pearson & Pearson, 1913, pp. 30–33). It is believed that the site was used for burials prior to becoming the officially recognized burial ground for the community. Like Boston and other Puritan settlements, cattle were permitted to graze on the grounds, disrupting and damaging early gravestones (Pearson & Pearson, 1913, p. 53). Although Maine settled relatively early with an attempt by the Virginia Company to establish the Popham Colony at Fort St. George II, permanent settlements were not established until around 1630 with the founding of York on the banks of the

York River. York was primarily made up of Anglicans, and an Anglican chapel and churchyard were constructed in the 1630s in the north of the village. However, in the mid-seventeenth century, the Massachusetts Bay Company purchased the claim to the Maine territory and a Puritan-style burial ground was established to the north–west of York Harbour (Emerson Baker, personal communication, April 6, 2016). The Popham Colony was established in 1607, in an attempt by the English to hold the coast of what is now the United States of America from the French, who occupied much of Atlantic Canada during the seventeenth century. While no graves have been identified at the colony thus far, thanks to John Hunt's highly accurate map of the settlement, we know that a 'Chapell' was constructed on a low elevated area with a planned bounded churchyard surrounding the building. While the financier, George Popham, died at the colony during its single year of occupation and it is likely he was interred in his settlement, the location of his grave has yet to be identified (Brain, 2016, pp. 17–40).

While much of Atlantic Canada, such as present-day Nova Scotia, was occupied by the French into the eighteenth century, the 'English Shore' of eastern Newfoundland was no stranger to British settlement. Prior to the seventeenth century, seasonal fishers and whalers lived and worked on the shores of Newfoundland and Labrador since the early sixteenth century (Ingstad, 1985). It was not until 1610, with the foundation of John Guy's Cupids Plantation (Cuper's Cove), that the British attempted the first permanent settlement on the rugged shores of the 'Rock' (Cell, 1969, 1982). Cupids was the first permanent British settlement in Newfoundland and what is now Canada and was partially surrounded by stone fortifications with three cannons to defend the inhabitants from pirate attacks (Gilbert, 2003, p. 118). While a burial ground has been identified at the settlement, marked with fieldstones and two imported eighteenth century headstones, it has been suggested that the narrow width of some of the graves could indicate seventeenth century burials (Gilbert, 2013, p. 84). However, this date has yet to be confirmed, and as was discussed in Chapter 3, the shape of a grave shaft does not directly correlate with the contents of the grave.

Many burial grounds in colonial Newfoundland date to the early–mid eighteenth century but based on the archaeological and documentary resources available for many settlements push the date of their settlement back into the seventeenth century. Unfortunately, information on seventeenth century burial grounds in Newfoundland is less readily available, in that a seventeenth century British burial ground in has yet to be identified and confirmed within the province. Documentary evidence at Cupids describes deaths at the settlement throughout the 1600s; however, while funerals are occasionally mention, there is nothing written about the burials themselves. The 1621 settlement of Ferryland, on the east coast of the Avalon Peninsula, is located about an hour south of the present-day capital of St. John's. Historic records and the discovery of three gravestone fragments during archaeological excavations in the 1990s provide some information on deaths within the settlement during the early seventeenth century and that a burial landscape was established to warrant the carving of gravestones from local slate (Lacy, Gaulton, & Stephen, 2018). However, no map of the settlement has ever indicated a burial space, nor have the excavations unearthed evidence of graves to date. At both Cupids and Ferryland, efforts to locate early burials are ongoing. Other eighteenth century burial grounds along the English Shore share similar traits such as being elevated within their settlements, burials on sloped landforms facing the ocean and very often the early sites were not associated with a church due to the lack of an established and permanent clergy in Newfoundland until the 1800s

(Pocius, 1986, p. 26). A reference study was conducted on 20 burial grounds in Newfoundland, to gain a better understanding of the eighteenth century burial landscape on the island and to provide a base of understanding in the instance that seventeenth century burials are identified at a colonial site. These sites were also chosen due to the likelihood that they predate the eighteenth century, when examining settlement patterns and census records from the area.

While obvious patterns between the sites used in this study can be drawn without looking too closely at statistical data, it takes a more nuanced understanding of the backgrounds of the individuals who made up each settlement to create a well-rounded image of their relationship with the dead. Folk traditions were upheld in some areas, protective marks on gravestones can be seen throughout the colonial Atlantic coast, and in Newfoundland, burials not only usually overlooked water but the dead *had* to be facing the sea, and it was said to be unlucky to remove things from a burial site, such as berries (Pocius, 1986). The burial landscape of colonial North America is as rich and active today as it was 400 years prior, remaining an important key to the study of early European settlers.

STATISTICAL ANALYSIS OF BURIAL GROUND ORGANIZATION

The analysis of this research was conducted with the goal of characterizing burial ground placement in early colonial settlements. It should be said from the start that this analysis originally looked at coastal British settlements and does not account for sites located inland away from the ocean or a shipping river, nor does it include family burial plots. This preliminary study was applied to the case study of Ferryland, with the results used to help guide 10 weeks of excavations in search of the early seventeenth century burial ground at the eastern Atlantic settlement. The parameters were chosen in order to encompass the earliest colonial settlements along the eastern seaboard. As well as informing the Ferryland excavation, to be discussed in detail in the following chapter of this volume, the results of this analysis may have the potential to inform on burial ground locations in other seventeenth century settlements, in conjunction with archaeological evidence and historical documentation.

The first statistical analysis of burial ground organization within this study area was conducted by John L. Brooke in 1988, where he examined burial organization and relationship to communities in over 80 different sites in Middlesex and Worcester Counties, Massachusetts (Brooke, 1988). Although his research primarily focuses on sites from 1730–1790, his examination of burial ground relationship to meeting houses includes sites from 1630–1730, covering the time period and portions of the study area observed in this study. Brooke's results show that the majority of burial grounds founded prior to 1673, his turnaround date for changing from strictly Puritan burial practices to include more Anglican and other traditions to 'take the place of that destroyed by the reforming impulses of early Puritanism' were separated from their meeting house overall (87%), but by the 1670s, burial grounds were reassociated with meeting houses/churches (Brooke, 1988, p. 464). This had to do with newer towns established in the 1670s onwards constructing their meeting houses directly beside burial grounds or older settlements building new meeting houses directly adjacent to or on top of older burial grounds. He also comments that early seventeenth century settlements had clear town centres, but that many groups buried their dead without ceremony outside of the centre of the community (Brooke, 1988, p. 465). Based on the results discussed below, Puritans along the east coast did not entirely separate their burial spaces from the heart of their communities, but pushed them to the periphery of ceremony all the same, with the removal of church-related prayer and funeral services. The separation of public spaces, in this case the meeting house or church and the burial ground, is all too apparent.

As stated earlier in this chapter, this analysis included 40 burial grounds from Hampton, Virginia, to the Popham Colony in Maine, with sites in Virginia, Maryland, Connecticut, Rhode Island, Massachusetts, New Hampshire and Maine. Due to the seventeenth century French populations in eastern Canada and the southern United States, and the Dutch occupation in the Pennsylvania and New York state, these areas have not been included in this study. The author intends to continue this research in the future and include these regions and cultural groups. The additional 20 sites explored in Newfoundland primarily date to eighteenth century and aid in the study of landscape exploitation and traditions in early British and Irish settlements in Newfoundland. Both studies facilitate a more comprehensive examination of the burial landscapes in their regions during a developmental period and could aid in the future when examining other underresearched settlements.

In order to analyze the settlements, a combination of visual spatial data collected through historic maps, documents, accounts and Google Earth Pro were employed to track down the earliest iteration of each settlement and its layout and the seventeenth century organized burial ground(s) within that layout. The data collection were based around a series of questions, answered for every site studied to ensure standardization of variables throughout the research. The following questions were used to organize the spatial data for each burial ground and were answered with either *yes, no* or *unknown*:

- *Was the site surrounded by fortifications:* This question asks whether a settlement had been partially or surrounded by fortifications such as a wall, palisade, ditch and embankment, towers or other manufactured earthworks.

- *If fortified, were the burials placed inside the fortifications:* This question was particularly important to the analyses, as walls are a defining aspect of a settlement. Walls are meant to protect the community, and going outside was sometimes dangerous for settlers. Were burials kept inside or moved outside of these walls?

- *Was the burial ground associated with a church or meeting house:* By 'associated with', the intention was to explore sites that had been constructed in conjunction (through records or visuals) with a church or meeting house on the same property or directly adjacent to the burial ground. The English churchyard model shows us a Parish church or chapel surrounded by graves in most cases, and it is well known that some dissenter groups in the sixteenth and seventeenth centuries disagreed with that association.

- *Was the burial ground on elevated land from the rest of the settlement area:* Were the burials themselves placed on a slope or elevation that was likely unsuitable to other construction or habitation and thus used for graves? Hills are often the sites of graves because they are not ideal for farming or houses, and they provide drainage for the graves themselves.

- *Was the burial ground located in the centre of the original settlement layout, and if not, roughly which cardinal direction from the settlement was the burial ground located:* Previous research (Brooke, 1988) has stated that prior to 1673, the Puritan dead were pushed to the edges of their settlements, segregated from the living spaces. Were burial grounds really being kept out of the town centres, the heart of the communities, or were people still burying their dead close to home?

RESULTS OF THE ANALYSIS

These data were collected in Microsoft Excel and processed in the Statistical Package for the Social Sciences to run descriptive and crosstabulation analyses. Unknown data were entered as missing values. Descriptive analyses were run in several different groupings of sites, selected based on their region, in order to do cross-regional analysis as well as an overall view of the coastal burial landscape trends. All 40 seventeenth century burial grounds were examined, and frequencies and chi-square goodness of fit tests (testing equal percentages) were run on all variables resulting from the previously defined questions, such as if the settlement was fortified or not and whether burials were inside of the fortifications. p-values are given for valid chi-square goodness of fit tests that were significant, meaning that the categories of that variable did not have equal percentages. It should be noted that due to the small sample size and small cell sizes, some of the statistical tests could not be performed. However, looking at trends in the data can provide insight into the creation of the burial landscape. Results are shown in Tables 4.3–4.5, at the end of this chapter.

The results of the 40 sites together show that 77.5% of the settlements surveyed were unfortified, leaving only 22.5% surrounded by fortifications at or soon after their founding ($p = 0.001$). These data reflect the development of colonial power along the Atlantic coast of North America: as Britain gained a larger foothold, they no longer felt that they needed

Table 4.3. Frequency Analysis of Seventeenth Century Settlements (40 Sites).

Fortified:	77.5% no (31)	22.5% yes (9)
Burials inside Fortifications:	33.3% no (3)	66.7% yes (6)
Church association:	61.5% no (24)	38.5% (15)
Elevated:	37.5% no (15)	62.5% yes (25)
Direction (1 unknown):	43.6% centre (17)	10.3% south (4)
	56.4% N/S/E/W (22)	15.4% east (6)
	15.4% north (6)	15.4% west (6)
Water:	52.5% Atlantic (21)	47.5% rivers (19)

Table 4.4. Frequency Analysis for Comparison between Regions (31 Sites).

	Massachusetts (15):		Connecticut (11):		Virginia (5):	
Fortified:	80% no	20% yes	90.9% no	9.1% yes	60% no	40% yes
Burials inside:	66.7% no	33.3% yes (of 3 sites)	0% no	100% yes (of 1 site)	0% no	100% yes (of 2 sites)
Elevated:	26.7% no	73.3% yes	45.5% no	54.5% yes	80% no	20% yes
Church:	85.7% no	14.3% yes (1 missing)	72.7% no	27.3% yes	0% no	100% yes
Direction:	40% centre	26.7% north	45.5% centre	9.1% north	60% centre	20% east
	60% N/S/E/W	20% west 13.3% east	54.6% N/S/E/W	18.2% west 27.3% south	0% south	20% west

Table 4.5. Frequency Analysis of Settlements in Newfoundland, Seventeenth and Eighteenth Century (20 Sites).

Newfoundland (20):

Fortified:	95% no (19)	5% yes (1)
Elevated (1 unknown):	5.3% no (1)	94.7% yes (18)
Church association:	65% no (13)	35% yes (7)
Direction (1 unknown):	31.6% centre (6)	10.5% north (2)
	15.8% south (3)	21.1% east (4)
	21.1% west (4)	68.4% N/S/E/W (13)

walls around their homes. When looking solely at fortified sites prior to 1700, the results show that 66.7% of these sites placed their burials within the fortifications, and 33.3% removed the burials to outside the fortifications. It was expected that walls around the living quarters of a settlement would have a greater impact on where the space for the dead would be placed. It is also interesting to note in fortified settlements there is a nearly even split between association of burial ground and church, with 44.4 % no and 55.6% yes. This likely indicates the desire of some settlers to separate from their traditions, while other groups still practice the association of church and grave.

Fortified or not, throughout the seventeenth century, burial grounds tended to be placed on elevated terrain from the rest of the settlement area, with 66.7% of burial grounds elevated within fortified settlements and 61.3% elevated in nonfortified settlements, within the study area. The placement of burials on low hills or slopes in or near a settlement was a common practice. Looking at the direction of the burial grounds in relation to the settlement, overall 43.6% were located in a town centre, 15.4% each for north, east and west and 10.4% south ($p = 0.007$). It should be noted that there was a higher number of central burial grounds in unfortified settlements (46.7% unfortified vs 33.3% fortified).

Analyses were also done by the regions of Massachusetts, Connecticut, Virginia and the island of Newfoundland, to see if characteristics varied by location. The Massachusetts Bay Company's establishment of Boston sent predominantly Puritan settlers across the Atlantic, similar to the nearby settlements of Plymouth, New Haven and Guilford. These settlers had vastly different ideas of how to treat the church, the dead and the settlement compared with the settlers who arrived in Jamestown on the behalf of the Virginia Company, or later settlements in Virginia such as Williamsburg, Yorktown or Hampton, all of which displayed more 'traditional' church and churchyard methods of burial organization associated. Analysis of 15 sites in Massachusetts showed that it is less likely for settlements in that region to be fortified, with 20% of sites surveyed in the area having fortifications ($p = 0.02$). At these settlements, 66.7% of the burial grounds were outside of the fortifications. Only 14.3% of the Massachusetts burial grounds surveyed were directly associated with a church ($p = 0.008$), and this is unsurprising considering the settlers' background. 73.3% of sites were located on elevated landforms ($p = 0.071$). In addition, 40% of the burials were in the centre of the MA settlements, with 26.7% to the north, 20% to the west and 13.3 % located to the east of the town centre (60% total) (Table 4.4).

The 11 settlements in Connecticut were, according to the data, quite like those in Massachusetts, with 90.9% of sites surveyed not being surrounded by fortifications, leaving only a scant 9.1% fortified at the original construction of the towns ($p = 0.007$). 100% of the burial grounds at the fortified settlements were not inside the fortifications, showing a trend through predominately Puritan-occupied areas. Only 27.3% of burial grounds in CT were associated with churches, and 45.5% of the burials were in the centre of town with the rest distributed between 27.3% to the south, 18.2% to the west and 9.1% to the north (54.6% total). Compared to MA, where 73.3% of burials were elevated, in CT, elevated sites showed a rough 50/50 split as to whether they were elevated or not.

In contrast to the MA and CT sites, settlements in Virginia (5 sites) were found to be fortified more frequently at 40% of the sites surveyed. In this region, controlled by the Virginia Company, 100% of burial grounds at fortified sites were placed within these fortifications. 60% of sites surveyed being in a central location, and rest were broken up between 20% to the east and 20% to the west, the least variation of all the directional results of the survey. This could be a manifestation of the traditional English churchyard and settlement structure that was attempted in the Virginia colonies. Interestingly, 80% of sites were not elevated, in contrast with MA and CT.

In Newfoundland, the population at Ferryland was largely Anglican, with a few Catholics left after Calvert brought a group of Irish Catholics with him in 1628. The settlement was fortified during the first few years as indicated by both historical and archaeological evidence. It is likely that Ferryland's first Governor, Captain Edward Wynne, was responsible for deciding exactly where to build the fortifications shortly after coming ashore. The consideration of a future burial ground would have had to factor into the layout of the settlement and likely would have been decided prior to any deaths. If there were undocumented lives lost in the early days of settlement at Ferryland, the soon-to-be completed fortifications would have been one of the variables affecting the placement of the burial ground, as it would be for any colonial settlement, though less influential than previously assumed. At Jamestown, the first to die were buried against the walls of the settlement, until the first church was constructed in 1609 and burials took place within (Kelso, 2006, p. 50). Here, settlers were confined due to attacks from Indigenous people on the compound, which had been constructed upon arrival and had strict orders to hide their dead from the Indigenous peoples so burials were not placed outside the walls. Settlements in many other regions, however, did not have this external pressure and were able to consider whether they wished to place burials inside or outside the perimeter of their settlement, regardless of fortifications.

The Newfoundland data (20 sites) revealed no major surprises for the island, but strongly contrasted the mainland sites (Table 4.5). Fortifications were present for only 5% of the surveyed sites ($p = 0.000$). Due to the nature of the island, 94.7% of burial grounds were placed on elevated landforms ($p = 0.000$), a placement which became a standard for Newfoundland burials, and 35% of sites in the eighteenth century were associated with churches, due to the lack of an established church on the island. Many communities opened unconsecrated burial grounds for their communities well before the arrival of clergymen and organized faith. The placement of burial grounds in their settlements is less specific than that of Virginia, with 31.6% central, 21.1% to the east, 21.1% west, 15.8% south and 10.5% north (68.4% total). These results are likely more to do with the geographic arrangement of the harbours and buildable land than the preferred choices of the settlers.

The overall analysis and analysis by region provided a characterization of location of burial grounds on the northeast coast and island of Newfoundland. Some different patterns emerged from the regional analysis which makes sense since the North American coast was colonized by different groups from the British Isles. Their beliefs shaped their understanding of death and burial and can ultimately be seen reflected in their burial practices. This analysis looked specifically at British-founded settlements made up of settlers predominantly from not only England but also Wales, Ireland and Scotland. Due to the economic backing of British companies and individuals, we expect to see a predominantly English influence on settlement landscapes. However, this does not mean that all individuals creating these settlements came from the same political or religious backgrounds. In fact, they most certainly did not!

The hope was that the analysis would provide a method of locating burial grounds. While the results can be used to provide some clues (*i.e.*, elevated, central, inside/outside fortifications), and indeed were used to guide the excavation at Ferryland, more sites would be needed to be able to use multivariate models for prediction. Other variables could be incorporated into the model as well such as religion, political views, size of colony and number of males/females to name a few. The case studies in the following chapters will demonstrate the need to combine quantitative date with historical documentation, records and archaeology in order to build a more complete picture of the site and its burial landscape.

5

CASE STUDY: THE COLONY OF AVALON AT FERRYLAND, NEWFOUNDLAND

The island of Newfoundland has a rich history of burial traditions, created as an amalgamation of British, Irish and French traditions, among many others. The following case study will explore the colonial British settlement at Ferryland, Newfoundland, through an application of the statistical analysis of burial ground organization, combined with archaeological evidence and historical records to uncover the location of the earliest seventeenth century burial ground at the site.

The excavations at Ferryland have contributed greatly to archaeologists' knowledge and understanding of the early colonial world, and how settlers adapted to surroundings that they were often unprepared for. They adapted their way of living in some respects, and stuck fast to their traditions in others, and in the middle of all of this was how their dead were buried. At the heart of any community are practices to deal with death and burial, and the settlers in Newfoundland were no exception, although their earlier funeral practices remain somewhat of an open question.

Did they retain historically traditional practices from their homelands of England, Ireland and Wales, or did they change traditions to adapt to the new landscape and way of life they have created for themselves? Archaeological evidence attempts to shed some light on these questions, while examining the religious, social and political ties that the settlers had at Ferryland.

THE BRITISH AND IRISH IN SEVENTEENTH CENTURY NEWFOUNDLAND

Before Newfoundland was known to Europeans as a land rich in fish and timber, it was home to several groups of Indigenous peoples (Tuck, 1976). The native people of Newfoundland, the Beothuk, inhabited the island when it was first 'discovered by Europeans' (Marshall, 1989), and surviving records at the Cupids Plantation indicate that peaceful trade took place between those settlers and the Indigenous peoples on multiple occasions. Beothuk occupation is clear in the archaeological record long before the seasonal fishermen arrived, although a relationship between these fishermen and the Beothuk is not known (Gaulton, 2001, p. 20; Pastore, 1989, p. 57). While the Mi'kmaq people still reside in Newfoundland today, the Beothuk were driven to extinction. For this, and all studies in colonized spaces, it is important to recognize that the settlers in Newfoundland were moving into an environment where they were not the first people to inhabit or exploit the land. The results of colonization are ongoing, and something that archaeologists must work to bring awareness to, as inhabitants of stolen Indigenous territories.

Prior to the permanent European settlements on the island, Norse sailors lived for only a few years at L'Anse aux Meadows around 1000AD, and seasonal fishers and whalers lived and worked on the shores of Newfoundland and Labrador since the early sixteenth century (Ingstad, 1985). It was not until 1610, with the foundation of John Guy's plantation at Cupid's that the British attempted a permanent colony of the island (Cell, 1969, 1982). Only one year after ships landed at Plymouth, MA, the plantation at Ferryland, Newfoundland, was founded in 1621, as the endeavour of Sir George Calvert, the First Lord Baltimore.

George Calvert was well known during his life and after, as being a Catholic in a time of Catholic persecution, as well as for his and his family's role in the development of British settlements in Newfoundland and what would become the state of Maryland. While Calvert grew up in a Catholic household, he converted to the Anglican Church from 1592 until around 1624/25, well after the establishment of his Ferryland Colony (Krugler, 2004, pp. 69–76). While he maintained his Protestantism, or at least a Protestant façade, while working for the King he returned to Catholicism after losing his high-ranking position as Secretary to the British Government. This was due to political considerations and not, as is the popular belief, because he was suspected of having been secretly practicing Catholicism (Krugler, 2004, p. 69). Shortly after leaving the position, he announced his conversion to Catholicism (Krugler, 2004, p. 69), and his intention for his settlement, his 'Colony of Avalon', to be the first religiously tolerant colony in North America (Fig. 5.1).

'*Feryland* is as pleasant and as profitable a Harbour as any in the Land' (Wynne 1621 in Cell, 1982, p. 254). While this statement, made by Ferryland's first governor, conveniently left out the harsh reality of life on the exposed eastern coast of the Avalon Peninsula of Newfoundland, Ferryland was indeed an ideal location for a settlement, owing to its defensible location, sheltered inner harbour and proximity to nearby inshore cod stocks. Within one year of arrival in the

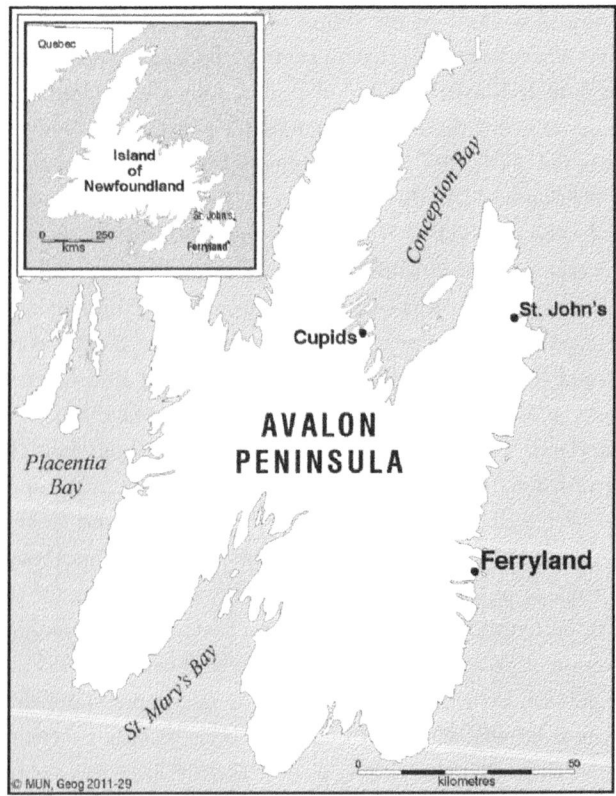

Source: Courtesy of Barry Gaulton, Ferryland Archaeology Project.

Fig. 5.1. Map Showing Context of Ferryland to St. John's and Cupids on the Avalon Peninsula, Newfoundland.

'coldest harbour in the land' as it is often referred to (Codignola, 1988), Governor Wynne and his settlers had constructed buildings and fortifications for the growing colony, including a cellar and the beginning of a garden (Wynne 1622 in Cell, 1982). It is likely that their immediate productivity was due to a predetermined plan for the settlement's development, coupled with the motivation provided by a fear of attack from French or Dutch forces, as well as pirates. The fortifications included a large ditch and earthen embankment, topped with a wooden palisade, and an earthwork hill that served as a bastion overlooking the only entrance to the harbour.

George Calvert himself finally visited the fledgling colony in the summer of 1627, and returned in 1628, bringing many Catholic settlers predominantly from Ireland, as well as members of his own family. The effects of the ongoing religious turmoil in the British Isles were felt in the Newfoundland settlements too, with the arrival of Catholics, and Calvert's goals of religious tolerance throughout the colony. While it is known that the settlers residing at Ferryland could, and did, openly follow the Catholic and Anglican Churches, this angered some members of the colony, such as the Anglican Reverend Erasmus Stourton (Krugler, 2004, pp. 97–99; Lahey, 1998, pp. 29–31). However, archaeological and documentary evidence at the settlement shows no evidence of a church structure having been built during Calvert's tenure of the Ferryland colony (Cruse 1667 in Pope, 1993). Instead the Mansion House, constructed specifically to accommodate Calvert and his family upon their arrival, was utilized for both Catholic and Anglican services, and later acted as a hospital during the winter of 1628/29 (Calvert 1629 in Cell, 1982; Lahey, 1998). In the eighteenth century, the Hylton Map of 1752 indicates a small building marked as a church and located near the Pool (the harbour) outside of the original settlement area, but there is no record of Calvert, nor the later proprietor Sir David Kirke ever having built a religious structure at Ferryland. The lack of a separated religious space at Ferryland is important when considering the spiritual organization of the area, as British churchyards were still in use back in the British Isles, but were slowly being given up for burial spaces outside of settlements as the result of dissenter reforms and growing health concerns.

While most burials in the British Isles, discounting death by suicide, lepers, burials at sea, etc., were buried in consecrated ground in England, only 38.5% of burial grounds in the seventeenth century British colonies surveyed had an established churchyard. This is assuming the definition that the place of burial is physically associated with the consecrated ground of a churchyard, and not located in a separate part of the settlement but still considered nonsecular. As no specifically religious structures had been built in Ferryland in the seventeenth century, early settlers were less likely to be concerned with interment in consecrated ground. This may be the result of Calvert's attempt to create a place of religious tolerance in the period between the Protestant Reformation and the English Civil War (approximately 1530s–1640s); by not having a church, nor a consecrated burial space, the space could be shared by members of faiths. Whatever the reason, the burial ground at Ferryland appears not to have survived in written records.

EVIDENCE OF DEATHS AT FERRYLAND

Nothing prepared George Calvert for the harsh nature of a Newfoundland winter, and in 1629, Calvert wrote to the King of England '*my howse hath been an hospital all this winter, of 100. persons 50. sick at a tyme, myself being one and nyne or ten of them dyed*' (Calvert 1629 in Cell, 1982). However, what Calvert did not include in his letter were the identities of the deceased, what they had suffered from and what happened to their bodies in the dead of winter. Both Catholics and Protestants placed importance on the burial of the physical body and commemoration in some way, and it is unusual that there is no trace of the burial ground on the landscape, either present or through historic records from later periods.

The only archaeological evidence of the burial ground comes from three gravestone fragments, from two slate gravestones. All found out of situ in the 1990s, one was uncovered at the bottom of the eastern defensive ditch, and the second gravestone (in two pieces) was associated with the renovation of the brewery and bake house (Carter, Gaulton, & Tuck, 1998, p. 57; Gaulton, 2006, p. 88). These gravestone fragments were not decorated, but bore well-carved inscriptions suggesting that at least one member of the colony had skill with stone lettering, likely one of the Welsh slators brought over for stone cutting. They invested the time into carving these commemorative stones. This is an indication of an organized burial space, for those two individuals as well as many more. One does not usually go through the trouble of carving gravestones in such an environment if they were not going to bury the bodies. The gravestones were carved from locally sourced stone at Ferryland, making them some of, if not the, *oldest* gravestones carved by British settlers in North America (Lacy, Gaulton, & Stephen, 2018).

The stones were found out of situ and broken, but buried in stratigraphy that dated to the early–mid seventeenth century. It is possible that Sir David Kirke, Governor of Newfoundland from 1637 until around 1653 (which he called the Poole Plantation), may have had a hand in disrupting the burial history at the site. Kirke was known to despise Catholics, and the Catholic association with Ferryland. Kirke himself may have ordered the eradication of the burial ground on the surface, by smashing the gravestones and potentially even constructing buildings over the area, as would have been seen as a Catholic space, despite the presence of Anglicans at the colony as well (see Gaulton, 2006, pp. 89–90). Such an action, though appearing sacrilegious, would have been in line with the monument destruction during the Reformation in the British Isles. As a result, this theory is not surprising, but has yet to be definitively proven. A second possibility is that the gravestones were smashed during either the Dutch or French raids of Newfoundland's coastline settlements in the late seventeenth century, but this would have resulted in the gravestones being deposited in a later context. The gravestones themselves appear to have been deliberately destroyed and discarded, erasing the presence of the dead within that landscape. As a result, the burial ground's location faded from memory.

While local lore suggested that the burial ground was on the Downs, or the hill, that rises to the south of the colony, archaeological evidence comes only in the form of the gravestone fragments. Without much to go on and scant historical records, other means of investigation had to be employed in order to narrow down potential locations for excavation.

THE SEARCH FOR THE SEVENTEENTH CENTURY BURIALS AT FERRYLAND

In order to inform the excavation locations, the statistical analysis of seventeenth-century burial landscapes of British North America were examined for patterns which would indicate potential popular burial locations within a colonial settlement. Ferryland was used as the case study to explore the use of these data to inform an investigation in search of a burial space. This excavation, which took place over 10 weeks during the field seasons of 2016 and 2017, was the first systematic attempt to locate the earliest organized burial ground associated with the Calvert-period occupation at the site; the 1620s.

Through examination of the results of the statistical analysis, in conjunction with local knowledge of the site and archaeological and historical evidence, it was determined that the most likely location for an organized burial at Ferryland would be to the east or south, outside of the fortified settlement, or in a central location within the walls. Probability indicated that the burials were likely on an elevated landform, without association to a religious structure. 61.5% of the burial grounds surveyed were not associated with a church, and according to surviving documents from Ferryland, there are no records of a church at the site, but that both Protestant and Catholic services were held under one roof (Wynne and Calvert letters, Cell, 1982). In 1630, it was reported to Rome that

> ...as to religious usage, under one and the same roof of Calvert, in one are Mass was said according to Catholic rite, while in another the heretics carried out their own

(Lahey, 1998, p. 29).

Previous excavations surrounding the Mansion House have revealed no grave shafts tucked against the walls, so that area was ruled out from further investigation.

The data showed that out of the 40 sites surveyed along the northeast seaboard prior to 1700, 43.6% had their burials placed close to the centre of the settlement, with 56.4% split between the cardinal directions, with 15.4% each to the east, north and west, and 10.3% to the south. However, according to local knowledge, along with the potential for the gravestones to have fallen or been thrown north off the hill, the south is a more likely location at Ferryland based on geographic and archaeological factors. Exploration to the north at Ferryland would run into an eroding sandbar or the ocean, and excavations to the west of the site are not possible at the time of writing, as that portion of the site is currently located under several contemporary buildings. Regardless of regional breakdown, elevated landforms are the most popular place to put a burial ground, geography allowing. It was not a common custom in the seventeenth century to sequester the dead too far away, out of sight and mind of those still interacting with the living portions of the settlement, so an area closer to the settlement would be more likely than not.

It has long been suggested that the seventeenth century burial ground was to the east of the settlement, directly outside the fortifications and between the current garden and the defensive ditch (Carter et al., 1998, p. 58). This theory was largely based on modern pictorial representations of the settlement in the 1620s and was largely based on the presence of the gravestone fragments found nearby. This part of the site had not been excavated prior to 2016 and was selected as part of this fieldwork investigation. In 2016, two areas to the east of the fortifications and two to the south were selected for intensive investigation through ground penetrating radar (GPR) scanning. GPR is used in various scientific disciplines such as archaeology and geology to gain a better understanding of what is below the surface, without having to disturbing the ground. The GPR transmits high-frequency radar waves from an antenna while being pushed and pulled along the surface of the ground, and measures the time it takes for these waves to transmit from and reflect back to the machine (Conyers, 2004, p. 1). Graves have successfully been identified with GPR across the world, but after nearly 400 years of laying in the acidic soil of the Avalon Peninsula, would there even be human remains left to excavate, much less identify with a GPR? GPRs can identify not only the location of a buried object but can also discern visible disruption amongst the soil layers. Grave shafts could be identified, even if the remains themselves could not.

The GPR survey utilizing a 500MHz Noggin Smart Cart from Sensors and Software, identified several anomalies of interest. Transects were run in a grid at 25 cm intervals, so as not to miss even the smallest of graves. Trenches were then

Case Study: The Colony of Avalon at Ferryland

laid out running north–south to cross-cut these anomalies to the east and south of the settlement area, in order to increase our chances of overlapping with a traditional Christian burial, which would be expected to run east–west (Fig. 5.2). As mentioned earlier in this text, historical period graves were often only a few feet below the surface, so we were not looking for evidence of disturbances too far down. The goal of this project was to locate grave shafts, not to disturb or exhume any human remains. In order to locate these graves without disturbing the burials themselves, excavations were conducted down to the glacially deposited subsoil layer to look for evidence that something had been cut *into* that layer. Because human activity will not exist below this layer, we can expect deeper soil features to cross-cut it, such a post holes or graves. At Ferryland, the subsoil is 40–70 cm below surface in

Source: photo by author.

Fig. 5.2. The Ferryland Pool (Harbour) Facing West from the Bastion.

most areas, so features that might have been disturbed by gardens above would still be partially preserved in the subsoil.

In order to create a feature, there must be a disturbance in the soil. A tree root can create a feature, as can a rabbit hole, or humans digging post holes or graves. When a grave is dug, the soil that is removed usually sits on the surface for a period, mixes together, and if it is rainy or windy, loses some of its initial composition. The stratigraphy of the subsurface is preserved in the side walls of the grave shaft, but the soil and sediments removed have been churned together. After the body or bodies are placed into the grave, this mixture of soil is put back into the grave. The texture, composition and even the sound against a trowel will now be different than the surrounding ground, helping archaeologists identify the size and shape of the grave itself.

To the east of the fortified settlement, trenches over the anomalies identified several post holes, created by wood posts being placed in the ground and eventually decomposing in situ, changing the chemical composition of the soil, as well as modern disturbances including back-hoe bucket scars which closely resembled graves upon first inspection Unfortunately, ground-truthing these areas, located to the east and west of the 'kitchen garden' on site today, lacked evidence of graves. However, one of the trenches revealed a large quantity of slate chippings and broken roof tiles, suggesting that a slator has prepared roof tiles for a structure near that location. South of the settlement on the hill just behind the most southern structures, trenches did not identify any evidence of burials either, but one 5 m trench cross-cut a feature that was identified as the southern defensive ditch and sod embankment, constructed in 1621/22 as one of the first projects of Wynne's earliest settlers. This was an exciting moment for the project, as it drove home the point that even if you are not finding what you thought you would, all data collected whether negative or positive as it pertains to your question are still data that are important for understanding the overall picture of the settlement, and its inhabitants. The identification of this ditch meant that the entirety of the south hill's edge could be discounted, as we know the ditch and embankment ringed the community.

Undeterred, the team began an off-set-grid testpit survey of a large field to the south of the defensive ditch, which had not been previously excavated, coupled with testpitting along the southeast terraces as well. These testpits were used to identify the depth to subsoil. Archaeologists see this as the stopping point. A back-hoe was brought into the site to open up eight trenches just above subsoil so we could get a better understanding of the landscape, and to see if graves were present on the hill slope. While we did not identify any graves within this portion of the site, a late seventeenth century deposit of high-status goods was uncovered, further explored by Dr Barry Gaulton of Memorial University of Newfoundland in 2017 and 2018. Previously it has not been known that people were living that far from the fortifications of the settlement during that period.

During the 2017 field season, which took place during a four-week period, excavations were focussed within the fortified settlement. As the result of ongoing excavations for decades at Ferryland, much of the interior settlement area was previously excavated; however, spaces near the brew and bake house where the gravestones were found were known to have been a 'town green', and terraces to the north were previously unexcavated. We were unable to use GPR within the fortified settlement due to the amount of stone rubble below the surface. In 1995, a reconnaissance radar survey took place at Ferryland in search of stone constructions and cobblestones, materials which produce high-contrast readings on the machine. The report of this survey suggested several areas for further investigation; however, the overall report appears to have resulted in rather busy data that are only useful in select locations, as the amount of stone in the subsurface distorts the reading (Deemer, 1995). As a result, GPR survey was deemed unreliable within the 'living' area of the fortified settlement, and ground-truthing commenced. A series of four trenches were opened surrounding the brew and bake house: one directly south on the hill slope, one to the west through the centre of the 'Kirke House', and two through the open 'green'. The trench in the Kirke House was placed with some cheek, as myself and Dr Gaulton could not help but wonder if David Kirke would have been so bold as to not only potentially break the gravestones and erase the burial space but to place his house overtop of the burials themselves. Happily, we did not find the burials under that structure.

None of the trenches opened in this immediate area uncovered evidence of grave shafts, although to the south of the brew and bake house, a pile of rubble was uncovered with a portion of a clay bread oven within it, dating to the period of reconstruction when Kirke had the building attached to the house as the kitchen. This rubble was in situ in a mid-seventeenth century soil layer, where a portion of the wall and ovens had been pushed over to the south of the slate structure, and several diagnostic pipe bowls were uncovered in the vicinity.

An additional two trenches were opened on the bastion earthwork, the highest point of the fortifications, on a gently sloped terrace at the north face of the structure. From previous excavations, we knew that the bastion was not a natural hill, and thus the interior structure may have been less densely packed, and thus be the first part of the earth surrounding the town to thaw in the spring. The trenches, however, quickly revealed to the team that the bastion was not made from earth and stacked sods as we had expected, but instead from layers of stacked sods and rocks, gravels to cobble-sized rounded rocks that must have been carried up the hill from the harbour area, an impressive feat. After trenches passed the safe-depth point and several steps had to be carved out of the hill, the 'bottom' or the natural hill had not yet been reached and it was determined that the chances of finding burials on the bastion slope were slim. This excavation expanded our understanding of seventeenth century earthwork construction, as well as a greater understanding of the effort exerted by those early settlers working to build the earthworks which surrounded the settlement.

While the excavations at Ferryland in 2016 and 2017 did not identify the location of the earliest burial ground associated with the Calvert period of occupation at the Colony of Avalon, the fieldwork itself provided valuable insight into the way in which the colony's settlers were exploiting their adopted landscape. Understanding the extent of features at the site, such as the ditch and palisade, expands the knowledge of why certain areas were not favoured for burials and affords archaeologists a clearer picture of the views and landscapes through the eyes of the seventeenth century settler. All information on building placement, gardens, buried ditches, slate chippings and more is information which builds the story of Ferryland in the 1620s. The excavations also identified locations that were suitable for graves but were not chosen to hold them. Because this research was the first systematic attempt to locate the early seventeenth century burial ground, knowing where the burials are not is invaluable information for anyone undertaking future research and excavations at Ferryland in the future.

Although the results of this case study did not yield the location of human burials, the study is not considered a failure, but rather an example of the use of a statistical model on a site when does not work with the model. Nevertheless, the data collected throughout the project are an advancement in what we as archaeologists know about burial settlement organization in the early seventeenth century, and indeed throughout the century. In the following section, we will explore an example of these data being applied to another early seventeenth century settlement, to show how it can be used to yield positive results.

ADDITIONAL CASE STUDY: GUILFORD, CONNECTICUT

Negative data are data. Statistics can only do so much, as the case study at Ferryland has demonstrated, in defining human behaviour. People are inherently difficult to quantify, and even though a society is guided by specific practices or ceremonies, there are always going to be factors, and people, who do not follow those guidelines. The results produced by the preliminary statistical research on seventeenth century burial grounds were not statistically significant when examined as one group, and even when divided into religious or region groupings, only some of the results proved particularly significant (Newfoundland's over 90% choice for elevated ground, for example). While these results can guide research into burial ground locations by indicating more probable placements within settlements, they should be considered in conjunction with archaeological, documentary evidence, and oral histories if possible, in order to collect as much information as possible prior to ground-truthing. This will reduce the risk of disturbing subsoil that could otherwise have been preserved.

In order to provide additional results for these data, the results of the statistical analysis were applied along with numerous lines of evidence to 'locate' a burial ground in a hypothetical case study.

Guilford, Connecticut

The small, seaside settlement of Guilford, CT, is a picturesque colonial town founded in 1639. The earliest settlers were Puritan, arriving just after the period of 'Great Migration' into the Massachusetts Bay area, and part of the wave of Puritan, Calvinist, and later Anglican settlers arriving in the region. Guilford was originally organized as blocks of land surrounding a large central 'village green', and the settlers may have based their town plan on that of the nearby town of New Haven, with the open green in the centre used for buildings, markets and all manner of activities (Bloomer, 1994, p. 58; Smith, 1877, p. 37). Henry Whitfield led the settlers to the site, originally called Menunkatucket, which is on the traditional lands of the Quinnipiac and Hammonasset's people (native-land.ca). His house is still standing as a heritage site in Guilford and is the oldest stone house still standing in Connecticut, built the same year that the settlement was founded.

For the first several years of the town, activities centred around the town green, which looked much like it does today, with trees and open grass. No buildings were initially constructed on the Green, but as an unfortified farming community the settlers felt like they needed more protection, and joined the already-established 'New Haven Colony'. As a result, the town was forced to build a meeting house to act as a church. The meeting house was built on the northeast corner of the Green in 1643, just four years after the settlement had been established (Bloomer, 1994, p. 58).

The topography of Guilford is relatively level, owing to its location near the marshes and coastline of the Atlantic Ocean. This was a prime location to build a settlement, just inland from the coast to protect from exposure, but close enough to reap the benefits of a harbour. Agricultural land near the settlement allowed them to prosper, and the settlement itself remained unfortified under the protection of the New Haven Colony, fitting into the statistical analysis of the Connecticut area, where 90.9% of settlements were not fortified. To locate the burial ground in Guilford, one should apply a comparison to the examples from Connecticut first, then look at the overall results for the seventeenth century. These data would suggest that elevated areas were only 9.1% more frequent in settlements in the CT region, but that 72.7% of settlements did not associate their burial grounds with a church initially. It is clear that Guilford did not erect a meeting house or church until 1643, and it is likely that settlers had died during those first 4 years, indicating that the burial space set aside by the earliest Puritan settlers would predate the meeting house. In term of directionality, 45.5% of burial grounds in the centre of town, 27.3% to the south, 18.2% west and 9.1% north of the settlements in the region. These numbers are skewed away from the south overall, but CT settlements appears to have used the southern locations more frequently than other noncentral placements.

Through historical research of the settlement, it is apparent that the settlement was partially designed after the layout of New Haven, CT. A famous fact about the town of New Haven is that their central town Green was used as the first burial ground, and that the gravestones were moved later to be housed in the basement of a nearby church. As almost half of the burial grounds in the region were located in the centre of the settlements, and given Guilford's association with New Haven, the most likely place to look for early seventeenth century burials would be in the town green itself, which is still present today as a 'well preserved village green [as a] chief attraction' (Sexton, 2002, p. 1).

The Guilford Green was indeed used as a burial ground, laid out as part of the original intent of the Green in 1639. Burials took place in the centre of the Green (Smith, 1877, p. 37), and predated the construction of the meeting house, which was not intended to be associated with the space originally (Bloomer, 1994, p. 58). The burial ground and the Green were not bounded by a fence, and the space was an active part of the daily community, eventually home to several structures including a blacksmith's shop, markets, school, churches and sometimes livestock (Dwight, 1823; Sexton, 2002). However, as the relationship with death in colonial settlements evolved, people began to become uneasy with the burials in the centre of the town and believed that the Green was becoming overcrowded and unattractive. These concerns are echoed by nineteenth century academic and writer Timothy Dwight in his memoirs, when he passed through the settlement in 1800. He lamented that:

> *...this square, like that in New Haven, is deformed by a burying ground, and to add to the deformity, is unenclosed. Instead of producing those solemn thoughts, and encouraging those moral propensities, which it was intended to inspire it renders death and the grave such familiar objects to the eye, as to prevent them from awakening any serious regard... Nor is it unreasonable to suppose, that the proximity of these sepulchral fields to human habitations is injurious to health.*
>
> (Dwight, 1823).

This sentiment was echoed in 1877 by Smith, who wrote that

> *...the ground was originally uneven and disfigured with numerous basins or pond holes, the central part had been injudiciously used for a grave yard, like the western portion of the public square of New Haven.*
> (Smith, 1877, p. 37).

Source: First Congregational Church after the Hurricane of 1938, c. 1938. Edith B. Nettleton Historical Room at the Guilford Free Library, Guilford, CT.

Fig. 5.3. Image of the Guilford Green after the 1938 Hurricane, with Uprooted Trees.

Dwight's memoirs reflect the decision to erase the burial ground from the settlement's landscape. By 1817, all the gravestones and monuments had been removed from the Green and relocated to a newly created burial ground outside of town, with the uneven ground levelled by 1824 (Bloomer, 1994, p. 60; Sexton, 2002, p. 4; Smith, 1877, pp. 37–38). The last of the buildings were razed from the Green by 1838, but not before the entire space was enclosed by a white wooden fence a year earlier, ending the uninhibited movement across the space that had been allowed for over 200 years (Smith, 1877, p. 38). The burials themselves were never relocated (Dee, 1998), and no heritage plaques around the edge of the park today mention the fact that the area was once used as the earliest burial ground by the town's founders, nor do they suggest that the burials themselves are still, for the most part, there. When a great storm hits the area and a tree is uprooted, there is always the chance that the roots could contain human remains, just as the hurricane of 1938 revealed when over half of the elm trees on the Green were uprooted and the graves below exposed (Colby, 1996, p. 24) (Fig. 5.3).

6

DISCUSSION AND CONCLUSIONS

DISCUSSION

The long-held stereotype for seventeenth-century colonial settlements on the east coast is that burials surrounded the church in the centre of town much like they often did in England. However, the statistical analysis suggests that this arrangement represented a minority of early settlements founded by the British in North America. Many factors lead to the development of the early seventeenth century colonial burial landscape: political, religious and social elements, all of which factor into how burials are organized and oriented within the context of the wider landscape. The Protestant Reformation was one of these pressures and had great influence on the adaptations of British burial landscapes, both in the British Isles and North America during this period. The Reformation removed what is often considered as the medieval Catholic 'cult of the dead', and as a result, actions, ceremony and grave markers were dramatically altered.

There are always extreme reforms during a major cultural change like the Reformation. Catholics were no longer allowed to practice their burial rites, not bury their dead in what had previously been their consecrated ground. In addition to the removal of Catholic burial practices came a growing group of dissenters: strict Protestant practitioners, sometimes called Puritans. They believed that the prayers said for the dead had no effect on the soul's ability to get through Purgatory or into Heaven. If earthly prayer no longer had effect on the afterlife, then burial in consecrated ground would not have an effect either, and therefore advocated for 'burial grounds' free from consecration. Not everyone agreed with these most extreme reforms, and the Puritans faced years of oppression in the British Isles before they were granted the right to bury their own dead as they saw fit.

Those who did not stay in the British Isles were among the first British settlers to make the permanent move to North America, and with this move they were able to practice their beliefs as they were not permitted to do back home. The concept of the unconsecrated, municipal burial ground would take time to gain acceptance in England, but in a land free from the established Anglican Church for a time, there was an opportunity to become an established community within the growing seventeenth century landscape that founded the basis of settlements such as Boston, MA, and Hartford, CT. Of course, Puritans were not the only religious denomination to sail across the Atlantic during the early seventeenth century! The first major settlements established by the British were influenced directly by the Anglican Church: Jamestown, VA, and the Popham Colony, ME. These settlements were constructed with a central church, and churchyard in some instances. Other faiths were present in the landscape as well, including Catholics, Quakers, Baptists, Calvinists, Lutherans and other Christian factions.

This examination of burial spaces through their religious, political and social backgrounds allows glimpses into the origins of the settlement itself, and the reasoning behind the organization of the living and dead spaces. Where the burial ground was in relation to living and working spaces was clearly influenced by a society's social beliefs, relationship to church and state, and how that society dealt with mortality and burial at a given moment. While many active burial grounds are located on the outskirts of a settlement today, removed from spaces that are regularly seen and thought about by the living, this was a less common practice in the seventeenth century, although the fear of overcrowded burial grounds bringing illness began to develop in heavily populated areas towards the end of the century. It perpetuated a fear that persists today: the corpse as dangerous. Barring the individuals having died of certain infectious diseases such as Ebola, a dead body is not dangerous, and settlers in the seventeenth century would not only have been familiar with seeing the dead, but having their burial spaces near the living areas of a town meant that ruminating on their own mortality was a common theme.

As settlers moved into what they considered to be a new land, they brought with them fractured national faith, and their desire to keep the dead close at hand. They used their dead to make a place for themselves within a stolen landscape, to establish themselves in a way which has continued in North American settler communities to this day: an eternal resting place for the dead, physically asserting their ownership over the land. This idea is changing, as North America slowly realizes that we cannot use very acre of available land to house the dead, and some burial grounds, such as Les Jardins du Souvenir's Saint Paul Cemetery in Gatineau, Quebec, employ what is sometimes considered to be a more European model of 'grave recycling'. This involves removing a body from the ground to be cremated or reburied in a different location if a fee is not paid, or the family wishes to give up their lease of the grave, similar to what is done in places like Luxembourg where available land for traditional burials is scarce.

It is clear that the settlers brought their traditions with them into North America. Sir George Calvert, Ferryland's first proprietor, was raised Catholic but spent his schooling and career as a practicing Anglican before returning to Catholicism in 1625, four years after the founding of Ferryland. As the figure with due influence over the settlement, what sort of organization could we expect from someone with his background? The town itself is a wonder of colonial engineering with its deep ditch and palisade, a stone and sod earthwork bastion overlooking the harbour below and stone buildings throughout from locally quarried stone (Gaulton, 1997; Lacy, Gaulton, & Stephen, 2018; Spiwak, 2020). While no church was built in Ferryland during the seventeenth century, this was not because the inhabitants had rejected the formality of the church itself, but that Anglican and Catholic services were held in Calvert's Mansion House to promote tolerance within the colony. This was abhorrent to some of the inhabitants, who attempted to report this 'misconduct'. The settlement itself was unusual, and while it appears the first settlers arrived with some semblance of a plan, they were not following a model, per se, for a church and burial ground initially. That is not to say that there were not many settlements that were following a model, and through their examination in this text, we have seen what different regions and groups favoured in terms of the placement and treatment of their dead.

This research explored the relationship between burial grounds and their settlements, founded by the British on the east coast of North America during the seventeenth century. While the results of the analysis were not statistically significant, they do show that overall, there was some preference towards placing burials on elevated ground, not physically associated with a church unless they were early Anglican settlements, and that fortifications surrounding a settlement did not have an influence on the placement of the graves themselves. Within fortified settlements, the results were split 66.7% yes/33.3% no, as to whether the graves were placed within the settlement walls or outside. Some of the results were more significant when scaled down to at a regional level, with an overwhelming 94.7% of burials in Newfoundland having been located on elevated ground in comparison to the settlement. It was also established that the burials themselves were only slightly more likely to have been positioned away from the centre area of a settlement than they were to be in the centre, with 40% of burials in Massachusetts in a central location (60% noncentral), 45.5% in Connecticut (54.6% noncentral) and 60% percent in Virginia (40% noncentral).

While previous research stated that seventeenth century settlers (in Massachusetts) were deliberately separating the dead spaces from those of the living (Brooke, 1988), this research concludes that this was only partially the case. Although a larger percentage of burial grounds in all regions surveyed were not associated with the centre of the settlement save for Virginia, the burial grounds still were not relegated to the outskirts of the inhabited area, they were simply not as central as they once were. In fact, almost half of the burials were still located in central locations, showing that the dead still had an important role to play in their society after death, even if that society was staunchly Puritan. That does not mean that the dead were not also being pushed to the periphery in other ways. The removal of a church associated with burial grounds in many settlements was a change for many individuals and was used as a political statement, a break from the Anglican Church in settlements such as Boston, Hartford and Guilford (Hopkins, 2014). Rather than being governed by the church, burial grounds in these settlements were often established as municipal, accessible by all and devoid of holy presence for many years (Hopkins, 2014, p. 27).

Access to, and interaction with, burial spaces was important to settlers, as demonstrated in Guilford, CT. The town's central burial ground was not enclosed by a fence or wall, and graves were interspersed with grazing cattle and settlers walking through the space, unperturbed by the burials beneath their feet and perhaps remembering a loved one or ruminating on their own mortality as they went. Graves were a common sight in the seventeenth century, especially to those living in colonial settlements where they were unfamiliar with the environments, perhaps were not living in the best conditions, and experienced greater violence that they might expect back home. That does not mean they wanted to hide the graves. Even when Boston's 1645 map in the Book of Possessions did not label the burial ground known today as King's Chapel, that does not mean that the space itself was not central within the community and accessible to all. While these spaces were often the subject of disruption due to another church gaining traction in the settlement (in many Puritan settlements this was the Anglican Church, but alterations also came through the introduction of Baptist faith, among others), today they have for the most part returned to the public as accessible spaces. However, the way in which visitors almost revere and protect these historic sites, often with signage marking famous graves and fences or walls surrounding the site, in many ways goes against how their Puritan founders intended for the spaces to be treated.

FURTHER QUESTIONS AND DIRECTIONS

There is one major question that has arisen from this research, and as with any good research topic, many other questions on top of it. One of these questions comes from the case study itself: just where are the burials in Ferryland located, if not in the sites of highest popularity and frequency within the time period and background? Analysis of similar settlements combined with archaeological evidence and local oral history suggested that the graves would most likely be to the east or south of the colony, on an elevated piece of land. Local speculation, and the historic plaques at the site, suggests the graves were dug just east of the defensive ditch and palisade, between the ditch and the large kitchen garden. Several trenches were dug there, there are no graves except those to bury trash in the twentieth century. Through systematic survey and excavation, ever 'popular' location for burials at the site was crossed off, leaving the team slightly bewildered, with dirt-stained gloves and faces.

There are several options for what was done with the graves. One option is that the burials were simply placed in a less statistically likely location than those indicated by the model. The model itself suggested the more popular options, though there can be many variations. As previously mentioned, human nature is not strictly quantifiable, and the settlers at Ferryland were not operating under the same pretenses as their neighbours to the south. The results themselves, while not inaccurate, are not particularly statistically significant. This means that they do not account for a major piece of the population. Perhaps rather than to the west, the settlers buried their dead that spring of 1629, after the ground had thawed, to the west of the settlement on the peninsula. Just west of the current excavation area at Ferryland is currently sitting beneath two houses and is understandably not available for excavation. A portion of the site was partially covered at one point by another large house from the late twentieth century, and evidence of earlier houses has also been uncovered at different levels of the site, from a nineteenth century hearth south of the brew and bake house to an eighteenth century tavern south of the bastion on the Downs. It is possible that the burials were disturbed during later periods of construction or that they may have been buried much farther from the settlement than was initially expected, outside of the area currently available for excavation.

We should not discount the possibility that the burials have been destroyed by other means. The soil at Ferryland, and throughout the Avalon Peninsula, is very acidic, and while we were observing higher than expected rates of organic preservation in the form of wood and faunal remains from seventeenth century layers at the site during the 2017 excavation (a partially burned piece of wood was uncovered over 1 m below surface during the bastion excavation), that does not account for the rate of decomposition of human remains in such an environment. It is not known if the people at Ferryland were burying their dead in coffins, or shrouds, or perhaps with no burial dressings at all. Without the protection of a coffin, their remains would have decomposed even quicker.

Excavations at Foxtrap, Conception Bay South, in 2016 and 2017 uncovered 31 graves dating to the nineteenth century at the first fully excavated settler burial ground in the province (Grimes et al., 2018). Every one of the graves contains a coffin, but almost none of the wood remained, reduced to organic stains in the soil hinting at where the coffin had once been. As a result of the acidic soil conditions at the site, only 18 of the burials had identifiable human remains, and of those 18 burials preservation was poor (Grimes et al., 2018). In some cases, the position of the legs could be determined by the 'soil shadows' left in place by the decomposition of organic material into the surrounding sediment leaving an impression of the legs at the bottom of the grave shaft (Grimes et al., 2018). What is important to understand about this example is that the burials themselves were carried out in very similar conditions to those at Ferryland: elevated ground, near the ocean, within the community, and the site predated a church being constructed in the area. However, Foxtrap's settler burial ground was established sometime in the nineteenth century, 200 years later than the 1628/29 deaths at Ferryland, and yet there was almost nothing left of the remains buried there. It is very likely that unless an environmental anomaly was present at the time of burial in Ferryland, there is nothing left of the early settlers.

The most popular question asked by visitors during the case study excavations asked by visitors to the provincial historic site was 'could they have been buried at sea?' (Lacy, 2018). Despite popular belief on the subject, it is highly unlikely that early colonial settlers were conducting sea burials at any time of year, much less during the dead of a Newfoundland winter with half of the colonists sick at a time. In order to carry out a sea burial, a ship would have to sail out beyond the protection of the islands and Ferryland Head into rough exposed seas. They would have had to sail out far enough to ensure the corpses did not wash back into their harbour and maintaining the ship while conducting a funeral. The Anglican Book of Common Pray 1662 presents prayers for the burial of sailors at sea in special cases only, but states that burial on land was the only *acceptable* way for disposing of a body (Buchanan, 2015, p. 115), and it is suspected that Catholic practices around this time would have been similar.

George Popham died at his colony in Maine in 1608, and his grave was not located through archaeological excavations, leading to speculations that a sea burial was conducted instead. Popham also died in the winter, and a burial at sea was discounted due to the rough weather at that time of year (Brain, 2016, p. 15). The same reasoning applies to Ferryland. Furthermore, if the burials took place at sea, why go to all the trouble of carving gravestones which began with the classic seventeenth century line 'Here lies the body of...'? Most of the settlers who populated the Colony of Avalon in the late 1620s were not sailors, and burial at sea would have not only been fitting but would have gone against the belief that your body must be buried on land in preparation for the Resurrection. Burial at sea for colonial settlers would have been unrealistic in most cases, and Ferryland is no exception. It is much more likely that the bodies at Ferryland were kept in an unheated building until the ground had thawed enough in the spring for graves to be dug. It is common practice to employ the use of a 'dead house' for the storage and protection of bodies prior to the burial, and this tradition carries into recent years in Newfoundland and Labrador, as well as other parts of North America. It is likely that the same was done in 1628/29.

This research could easily be expanded upon by covering additional settlements of similar type and age, as well as moving farther inland from the Atlantic Ocean. An interesting comparison would be expanding the study to include early burial spaces from other religious groups, as well as other nationalities such as Dutch and French, who had a large presence on the east coast and into the Maritimes during the seventeenth century. Expanding the study parameters would allow a greater understanding of settler relationships with death and dying through their organization of burial spaces as compared to spaces for the living.

CONCLUSIONS

When this project began, the main goal was to inform the search for the burials of those who died in Ferryland, at the Colony of Avalon, in the 1620s. In order to understand trends in burial ground organization in the seventeenth century, similar communities had to be explored to build a picture of how the dead were buried, populations' relationships with the dead and the afterlife and how the church influenced their burial practices. The results were the first wide-scale study of spatial organization of seventeenth century British burial grounds in colonial North America. The sites covered through this research are not an exhaustive list of all sites from the period, but merely a preliminary study to show the potential advantages of such a survey and how it can add to an archaeological investigation into a historical settlement. The earliest seventeenth century colonial burial landscapes remain understudied, due to their often-invisible presence against a more dramatic historical backdrop. Early burial grounds were not filled with decorated gravestones, opting for plain inscribed stones, shaped or rough fieldstones or no markers at all. There is much we can learn from studying these early spaces of morbidity, through their organization within their settlements.

The statistical analysis shed light on the stereotypical American colonial ideal of a church surrounded by graves in the centre of town. Within the early 1600s landscape, this scene was in the minority, with 72.7% and 85.7% of burial grounds in Connecticut and Massachusetts, respectively, not having an association with a church when they were first established. Like-minded people often settled near one another, which decreases the likelihood of wild divergences in the spatial organization of burial grounds, something which relied as much on social cues as it did on geography. Even as Ferryland stands as a potential anomaly against the results of this model, it is clear through geologic testing of the gravestones uncovered at the site that the settlers at Ferryland were involved in creating a physical space to house their dead by carving their gravestone from locally quarried slate (Lacy et al., 2018).

The statistical analysis presented in this research was developed with the purpose of informing on likely locations at a site in order to narrow down a survey or excavation, and whether or not the resulting survey comes up with positive results, these results in no way lessen the efficiency of the model or the accuracy of the information contained within. It suggests that the people at Ferryland, when faced with a difficult winter and many deaths, may have had to resort to creating a burial spaced quickly and certainly in differing circumstances to other sites in surveyed. The additionally hypothetical case studies have shown that a combination of historical documentation and records combined with the results of the model would have had a positive effect in identifying the burial grounds in the sites discussed, had those burial grounds gone unnoticed until today.

The colonial burial landscape of seventeenth century British North America was developed out of a desire not only to explore what they considered new lands and push boundaries but also to instill ownership over a foreign land through the direct interment of human remains. By examining what is often a 'hidden' aspect of the burial landscapes, aspects of early colonial settlements are brought to light and with them, a greater understanding of not only how the colonists in North America lived and died centuries ago but also how our relationships with the dead has changed and grown since then.

REFERENCES

PRIMARY SOURCES

Baillie, M. (1812). On the embalming of dead bodies. *Transactions of a Society for the Improvement of Medical and Chirurgical Knowledge, 3*, 7–23.

Bain, A. (2010). Environmental and economic archaeologies of missions, colonies, and plantations. *Historic Archaeology, 44*(3), 1–3. [Electronic document]. Retrieved from http://www.jstor.org/stable/25762253, Accessed on August 1, 2017.

Benes, P. (1977). *The masks of orthodoxy: Folk gravestone carvings in Plymouth County, Massachusetts, 1689–1805.* Amherst, MA: University of Massachusetts Press.

British Library Board. (2017). *The dissolution of the Monasteries.* British Library, Learning English Timeline. [Website]. Retrieved from https://www.bl.uk/learning/timeline/item126620.html

Dwight, T. (1823). *Travels in New England and New York* (Vol. 2). Cambridge, MA: The Belknap Press of Harvard University Press.

Gaimster, D., & Gilchrist, R. (2003). *The archaeology of the reformation 1480–1580.* Leeds: Maney Publishing Ltd.

Guilford Free Library Archives. (1938). First congregational church after the hurricane of 1938 (Edith B. Nettleton Historical Room at the Guilford Free Library, Guilford, CT). Retrieved from http://archives.guilfordfreelibrary.org/items/show/58. (Reproduced with permission).

Haywood, S. (2019). Colonial expressions of identity in funerals, cemeteries and funeral monuments of nineteenth-century Perth, West Australia. *Genealogy, 2*(3), 23.

Houlbrooke, R. (1999). The age of decency: 1600–1760. In P. J. Jupp & C. Gittings (Eds.), *Death in England: An illustrated history* (pp. 174–201). Manchester: Manchester University Press.

Hutchinson, R. (2001). Tombs of brass are spent: Reformation reuse of monumental brasses. In D. Gaimster & R. Gilchrist (Eds.), *The archaeology of the reformation 1480–1580* (pp. 450–468). Leeds: Maney Publishing.

Kirke, D. (1639). *Letter to Archbishop Laud [from Ferryland]* (Transcribed by P. E. Pope,). Great Britain, PRO, Colonial Office, CO 1/10(40), 119. Retrieved from https://www.heritage.nf.ca/articles/exploration/david-kirke-letter-archbishop-1639.php

Mather, C. (1713). *A Christian funeral: A brief essay, on the case, what should be the behaviour of a Christian at a funeral? Or, some directions, how to regulate a funeral by the rules of religion; and how to enliven religion from the circumstances of the dead, at the house of mourning.* Boston, MA: Timothy Green. Retrieved from the Internet Archive.

Morton, N. (1669/1855). *New England's memorial* (6th ed.). Boston, MA: Congregational Board of Publication.

Norris, M. (1977). *Monumental brasses: The memorials.* London: Phillips and Page.

Order of the Good Death. (2019). *Natural burial (website).* Retrieved from http://www.orderofthegooddeath.com/resources/natural-burial#:~:text=Natural%20(or%20%E2%80%9Cgreen%E2%80%9D),protection%2C%20restoration%2C%20and%20management

Riordan, T. B.(1997). The 17th-century cemetery at St. Mary's City: Mortuary practices in the Early Chesapeake. *Historical Archaeology, 31*, 28–40. doi:10.1007/BF03374242

Rodwell, W. (1989). *The archaeology of religious places.* Philadelphia, PA: University of Pennsylvania Press.

Semple, S., & Williams, H. (2015). Landmarks of the dead: Exploring Anglo-Saxon mortuary geographies. In M. C. Hyer & G. R. Owen-Crocker (Eds.), *The material culture of the built environment in the Anglo-Saxon World, Vol. 2 of the material culture of daily living in the Anglo-Saxon World.* Liverpool: Liverpool University Press.

Sewall, S. (1697). The diary of Samuel Sewall, 1674–1729. M. Halsey Thomas (Ed.), *Newly edited from the manuscript at the Massachuetts Historical Society.* New York: Farrar, Straus and Giroux.

The Monumental Brass Society. (1988). *Monumental brasses: The portfolio plates of the monumental brass society 1894–1984.* Suffolk, NH: Boydell Press.

Virginia Company. (1606). *Instructions for the Virginia colony 1606.* University of Groningen, American History Documents [Electronic document]. Retrieved from http://www.let.rug.nl/usa/documents/1600-1650/instructions-for-the-virginia-colony-1606.php. Accessed on December 1, 2016.

Williams, D. (2019). *Map of the study area.* Created in GIS for publication, used with permission.

SECONDARY SOURCES

Anschuetz, K. F., Wilshusen, R. H., & Scheick, C. L. (2001). An archaeology of landscapes: Perspectives and directions. *Journal of Archaeological Research, 9*(2), 157–211.

Areta. (2018). A protection symbol for the home: The six-petal rosette on the crossbeams of Galicia. *Forgotten Galicia: Remnants of the Past Found in Lviv, Galicia & the Former Austrian Empire* [Electronic document]. Retrieved from https://forgottengalicia.com/a-protection-symbol-for-the-home-the-six-petal-rosette-on-the-crossbeams-of-galicia/. Accessed on March 4, 2019.

Augé, C. R. (2013). *Silent sentinels: Archaeology, magic, and the gendered control of domestic boundaries in New England, 1620–1725*. Thesis, dissertation, and professional papers. Paper 884: Doctor of philosophy in anthropology, cultural heritage studies. University of Montana, Missoula, MT.

Baker, E. W. (2018, October 3). Deliver us from evil: Counter-magic in early New England. Presentation, Salem, Massachusetts.

Bartram, A. (1978). *Tombstone lettering in the British Isles*. London: Lund Humphries.

Baugher, S., & Veit, R. F. (2014). *The archaeology of American cemeteries and gravemarkers*. Gainesville, FL: University Press of Florida.

Bayles, R. M. (1888). *History of Newport County, Rhode Island: From the year 1638 to the year 1887, including the settlement of its towns, and their subsequent progress*. New York, NY: L. E. Prestion. Retrieved from https://archive.org/details/historyofnewport00bayl

Becker, M. J. (2005). An update on colonial witch bottles. *Pennsylvania Archaeologist, 75*(2), 12–23.

Beirne, F. F. (1967). *St. Paul's Parish, Baltimore: A chronicle of the mother church*. Baltimore, MD: Horn-Shafer.

Bender, T. (1988). The "rural" cemetery movement: Urban travail and the appeal of nature. In R. B. St. George (Ed.), *Material life in America, 1600–1860* (pp. 505–518). Boston, MA: Northeastern University Press.

Binski, P. (1996). *Medieval death: Ritual and representation.* London: British Museum Press.

Blachowicz, J. (2006). *From slate to marble: Gravestone carving traditions in eastern Massachusetts, 1770–1870.* Evanston, IL: Graver Press.

Blake, S. L. (1897). *The early history of the first church of Christ, New London, Conn.* New London, CT: The Day Publishing Company. Retrieved from https://archive.org/details/earlyhistoryoffi00blak

Bloomer, N. (1994). Guilford, Connecticut: The Guilford green. *Places Journal, 9,* 56–65. [Electronic document]. Retrieved from http://escholarship.org/uc/item/8fc3x8mk. Accessed on June 6, 2017.

Brain, J. P. (2016). *Fort St. George II: Additional archaeological investigation of the 1607–1608 Popham colony* (Occasional publications in maine archaeology, No. 16). Augusta, ME: The Maine Historic Preservation Commission/The Maine Archaeology Society.

British Museum. (2019). *Tombstone of Gaius Saufeius* (Registration No. 1873,0521.1). British Museum, Department of Britain, Europe and Prehistory, London. Retrieved from https://www.britishmuseum.org/research/collection_online/collection_object_details.aspx?objectId=894339&partId=1&searchText=roman+lincoln&page=23

Brooke, J. L. (1988). "For honour and civil worship to any worth person": Burial, baptism, and community on the Massachusetts New Frontier, 1730–1790. In R. B. St. George

(Ed.), *Material life in America, 1600–1860* (pp. 463–485). Boston, MA: Northeastern University Press.

Buchanan, C. (2015). *Historical dictionary of Anglicanism* (2nd ed.). Lanham, MD: Rowman & Littlefield.

Buckham, S. (2003). Commemoration as an expression of personal relationships and group identities: A case study of York cemetery. *Mortality*, 8(2), 160–175.

Buckham, S. (2016). Not "architects of decay": The influence of graveyard management on Scottish burial landscapes. In S. Buckham, P. C. Jupp, & J. Rugg (Eds.), *Death in modern Scotland, 1855–1955: Beliefs, attitudes and practices* (pp. 215–240). Edinburgh: Peter Lang.

Carter, M., Gaulton, B., & Tuck, J. A. (1998). Archaeology at Ferryland, Newfoundland, 1997. *Avalon Chronicles*, 3, 49–62.

Cell, G. T. (1969). *English enterprise in Newfoundland 1577–1660*. Toronto: University of Toronto Press.

Cell, G. T. (Ed.). (1982). *Newfoundland discovered: English attempts at colonisation, 1610–1630*. London: The Hakluyt Society.

Center Church. (n.d.). *History of Center Church, The first Church of Christ in Hartford* [Electronic document]. Retrieved from http://www.centerchurchhartford.org/about.history.asp. Accessed on June 6, 2017.

Champion, M. (2015). *Medieval graffiti: The lost voices of England's Churches*. London: Ebury Press.

Cherryson, A. K. (2019). Dressing for the grave: The archaeological evidence for the preparation and presentation of the corpse in post-medieval England. In H. Mytum & L. Burgess (Eds.), *Death across oceans: Archaeology of coffins and vaults in Britain, America, and Australia* (pp. 37–56). Washington, DC: Smithsonian Institute.

Codignola, L. (1988). *The coldest harbour of the land: Simon Stock and Lord Baltimore's colony in Newfoundland, 1621–1649*. Montreal: McGill–Queen's University Press.

Colby, P. (1996). *Guilford and the Great New England Hurricane of 1938*. Guilford, CT: Guilford Paper Series.

Colonial Williamsburg Foundation. (2017). Bruton Parish churchyard. Colonial Williamsburg [Electronic document]. Retrieved from http://www.history.org/almanack/places/hb/hbbruyd.cfm. Accessed on September 18, 2017.

Conway, C. (2015). *Location map, Newfoundland settlements*. Image in: Custom-made ceramics, transatlantic business partnerships and entrepreneurial spirit in early modern Newfoundland: An examination of the SK vessels from Ferryland. *International Journal of Historical Archaeology, 19*, 3. (Courtesy of Barry Gaulton, Ferryland archaeology project).

Conyers, L. B. (2004). *Ground penetrating radar for archaeology*. Walnut Creek, CA: Altamira Press.

Corey, D. P. (1899). *The history of Malden, Massachusetts, 1633–1785*. Malden, MA: Author. Retrieved from https://archive.org/details/historymaldenma00coregoog

Curl, J. S. (2000). *The Victorian celebration of death*. Gloucestershire: Sutton (Reprint, 2001).

Curvers, J. (2010). *Burial rituals and the reformations in early modern Europe: A comparative study*. Master thesis comparative history. Utrecht University, Netherlands.

De Voragine, J. (1993). *The Golden Legend: Reading on the Saints* (Vol. 2). W. G. Ryan, Trans. Princeton, NJ: Princeton University Press.

Dee, J. E. (1998). Bones beneath your feet: Unmarked graves might be closer than you think. *Hartford Courant* [Electronic document]. Retrieved from http://articles.courant.com/1998-10-31/news/9810310176_1_prison-inmates-town-bones-beneath-your-feet. Accessed on June 6, 2017.

Deemer, S. (1995). *Reconnaissance radar survey in Ferryland*. Unpublished report. Earth Sciences Department, Memorial University of Newfoundland, St. John's, Newfoundland.

Deetz, J. (1977). *In small things forgotten: The archaeology of early American life*. New York, NY: Anchor Books.

Dethlefsen, E., & Deetz, J. (1966). Death's heads, cherubs, and willow trees: Experimental archaeology in colonial cemeteries. *American Antiquity, 31*(4), 502–510.

Duffy, E. (2005). *The stripping of the alters* (2nd ed.). New Haven, CT: Yale University Press.

Easton, T. (1999). Ritual marks on historic timber. *Weald & Downland Open Air Museum Journal*, Spring, pp. 22–35. Retrieved from http://www.wealddown.co.uk/wp-content/uploads/2014/10/1999-04-WDOAM-Magazine.pdf

Evans, I. (2011). Ritual marks and magic. *Trust News Australia*, May. (Cultural heritage). Retrieved from https://www.academia.edu/587206/Ritual_Marks_and_Magic.pdf

First Parish of Newbury. (2016). *History of the First Parish Church of Newbury* [Electronic document]. Retrieved from http://firstparishofnewbury.org/about-us/history/. Accessed on November 30, 2016.

Forbes, H. M. (1927). *Gravestones of early New England and the men who made them, 1653–1800*. New York, NY: Da Capo Press (Reprint, 1967).

Fossier, R. (2010). *The axe and the oath: Ordinary life in the middle ages*. L. G. Cochrane, Trans. Princeton, NJ/Oxford: Princeton University Press.

Francaviglia, R. V. (1971). The cemetery as an evolving cultural landscape. *Annals of the Association of American Geographers*, 61(3), 501–509.

Gaulton, B. (1997). *Seventeenth-century stone construction at Ferryland, Newfoundland (area C)*. Master of arts thesis, Department of Archaeology, Memorial University of Newfoundland, St. John's, Newfoundland.

Gaulton, B. (2006). *The archaeology of gentry life in seventeenth-century Ferryland*. PhD thesis, Department of Archaeology, Memorial University of Newfoundland, St. John's, Newfoundland.

Gaulton, B., & Miller, A. F. (2009). Edward Wynne's The Brittish India or a compendious discourse tending to advancement (circa 1630–1631). *Newfoundland and Labrador Studies*, 24(1), 111–120.

Gaulton, R. (2001). An early historic Beothuks occupation at Ferryland, Newfoundland. In J. A. Tuck & B. Gaulton (Eds.), *Avalon Chronicles* (Vol. 6, pp. 19–56). Ferryland: The Colony of Avalon Foundation.

Gilbert, W. (2003). Finding cupers cove. In J. A. Tuck & B. Gaulton (Eds.), *Avalon Chronicles: The English in America 1497–1696* (Vol. 8, pp. 117–154). Ferryland: The Colony of Avalon Foundation.

Gilbert, W. (2013, February). Excavations at Cupids (CjAh-13), 2012. In *Provincial archaeology office 2012 archaeology review* (Vol. 11, pp. 80–84). Ferryland: Department of Tourism, Culture, and Recreation. Retrieved from http://www.tcii.gov.nl.ca/pao/newsletters/pdf/Vol11-2012.pdf

Gittings, C. (1984). *Death, burial and the individual in early modern England*. London: Routledge.

Goodenough, E. R. (1957, January). The study of man: Pagan symbols in Jewish antiquity. *Commentary*. Retrieved from https://www.commentarymagazine.com/articles/the-study-of-man-pagan-symbols-in-jewish-antiquity/. Accessed on March 4, 2019.

Goodwin, S. (n.d.). Marblehead in the 1600's. *Slideshow for the Marblehead Museum and Historical Society* [Electronic document]. Retrieved from http://marbleheadmuseum.org/Marblehead_in_the_1600s.pdf. Accessed on June 6, 2017.

Graves, C. P. (2008). From an archaeology of iconoclasm to an anthropology of the body. *Current Anthropology, 49*(1), 35–60.

Grimes, V., Lear, M., Munkittrick, J., & Lacy, R. (2018). Excavation and preliminary analysis of a historical burial ground at Foxtrap-2 (CjAf-10). In *Provincial archaeology office annual review 2017*. Foxtrap, Newfoundland: Department of Tourism, Culture, Industry, and Innovation, Government of Newfoundland and Labrador. Retrieved from http://www.tcii.gov.nl.ca/pao/arch_in_nl/index.html

Hall, D. D. (1976). The gravestone image as puritan cultural code. In P. Benes (Ed.), *Puritan gravestone art* (pp. 23–32). Boston, MA: Boston University Press.

Harding, V. (1992). Burial choice and burial location in later medieval London. In S. Basset (Ed.), *Death in towns: Urban responses to the dying and the dead, 100–1600* (pp. 119–135). London: Leicester University Press.

Harding, V. (2003). Choices and changes: Death, burial and the English reformation. In D. Gaimster & R. Gilchrist (Eds.), *The archaeology of the reformation 1480–1580* (pp. 386–398). Leeds: Maney.

Hillerbrand, H. J. (Ed.). (1968). *The protestant reformation.* London: Macmillan.

Historic Jamestowne. (2018). The Knight's tombstone. *Jamestown Rediscovery: Historic Jamestowne.* Retrieved from https://historicjamestowne.org/archaeology/1617-church/knights-tomb/

Hoggard, B. (2019). *Magical house protection: The archaeology of counter-witchcraft.* New York, NY: Berghahn Books.

Hopkins, C. G. D. (2014). *The shadow of change: Politics and memory in New England's historic burying grounds, 1630–1776.* Unpublished doctoral dissertation, Department of American Studies, Harvard University, Boston, MA. Retrieved from https://dash.harvard.edu/handle/1/12274107

Houlbrooke, R. (1998). *Death, religion, and the family in England, 1480–1750.* Oxford: Clarendon Press.

Ingold, T. (1993). The temporality of landscape. *World Archaeology, Concepts of Time and Ancient Society, 25*(2), 152–174.

Ingstad, H. (1985). *The norse discovery of America, Vol. 2: The historical background and the evidence of the norse settlement discovered in Newfoundland.* Oslo: Norwegian University Press.

Justice Pinsent. (1888). The old graveyards. In *The Colonist Xmas number* (Vol. 3). Retrieved from http://collections.mun.ca/cdm/compoundobject/collection/cns_period/id/46463/rec/15?fbclid=IwAR0mdnWv3A_A-QBg5K_aNP4-kNdA3szkPYHEhSk0dB-SV-ornyAc-bfYfhM

Keene, M., Keene, P., & Auger, K. (1999). The grave site: Point of graves burial ground, graves, genealogy, ghosts.

Seacoast NH [Electronic document]. Retrieved from http://www.seacoastnh.com/dead/graves.html. Accessed on June 6, 2017.

Kelso, W. M. (2006). *Jamestown: The buried truth*. Charlottesville, VA/London: University of Virginia Press.

Kermode, P. M. C. (1907). *Manx crosses, or, the inscribed and sculptured monuments of the isle of man from about the end of the firth to the beginning of the thirteenth century*. London: Bemrose & Sons. Retrieved from http://www.isle-of-man.com/manxnotebook/fulltext/mc1907/index.htm

Killgrove, K. (2018). New Pompeii graffiti may rewrite history in a major way. *Forbes*, October 18. Retrieved from https://www.forbes.com/sites/kristinakillgrove/2018/10/16/new-pompeii-graffiti-may-rewrite-history-in-a-major-way/#541ec5f85484

Krugler, J. D. (2004). *English and Catholic: The Lords Baltimore in the seventeenth century*. Baltimore, MD/London: Johns Hopkins University Press.

Lacy, R. S. (2017a). *"Here lieth interr'd": An examination of 17th-century British burial landscapes in eastern North America*. Master of arts thesis, Department of Archaeology, Memorial University of Newfoundland, St. John's, Newfoundland. Retrieved from http://research.library.mun.ca/12933/1/thesis.pdf. (Available through Memorial University of Newfoundland, Queen Elizabeth II library).

Lacy, R. S. (2017b). Outsourcing monuments? – Gravestone carving vs. importation in Newfoundland. *Spade & the Grave*. Retrieved from https://spadeandthegrave.com/2017/05/26/outsourcing-monuments-gravestone-carving-vs-importation-in-newfoundland/

Lacy, R. S. (2018). Public engagement through burial landscapes: Cupids and Ferryland, Newfoundland. *AP: Online Journal of Public Archaeology*, Special volume 3: Death in the contemporary world: Perspectives from public archaeology, 55–78. Retrieved from http://revistas.jasarqueologia.es/index.php/APJournal/issue/view/14/showToc

Lacy, R. S., Gaulton, B. C., & Piercey, S. J. (2018). Inscriptions, outcrops, and XRF: Analysis of the Ferryland gravestones. *North Atlantic Archaeology Journal*, *5*, 91–110.

Lahey, R. J. (1998). The role of religion in Lord Baltimore's colonial enterprise. *Avalon Chronicles*, *3*, 19–48. (Reprinted from: *Maryland Historical Magazine*, 72(4), Winter 1977).

Linden-Ward, B. (1989). Strange but genteel pleasure grounds: Tourist and leisure uses of nineteenth-century rural cemeteries. In R. E. Meyer (Ed.), *Cemeteries and gravemarkers: Voices of American culture* (pp. 293–328). London: UMI Research Press.

Litten, J. (1992). *The English way of death: The common funeral since 1450*. London: Robert Hale (Reprint, 2002).

Love, Rev. W. D. L. (1914). *The colonial history of Hartford: Gathered from the original records*. Hartford, CT: Author. Retrieved from https://archive.org/details/colonialhistoryo00loverich

Ludwig, A. I. (1966). *Graven images*. Middletown, CT: Wesleyan University.

Manning, M. C. (2014). The material culture of ritual concealments in the United States. *Historical Archaeology*, *48*(3), 52–83.

Marshall, I. (1989). *The Beothuk of Newfoundland*. St. John's: Breakwater Books (Reprint, 2001).

Marshall, P. (2002). *Beliefs and the dead in reformation England*. Oxford: Oxford University Press.

Meeson, B. (2005). Ritual marks and graffiti: Curiosities or meaningful symbols? *Vernacular Architecture*, 26, 41–48.

Moody, A. C. (1935). The burial ground: The sons & daughters of the first settlers of Newbury, Massachusetts [Electronic document]. Retrieved from https://www.sonsanddaughtersofnewbury.org/the-burial-ground. Accessed on June 6, 2017.

Museum of Fine Arts. (2018). *Harp (Cláirseach)*. Boston, MA: Leslie Lindsey Mason Collection: Museum of Fine Arts. Retrieved from https://www.mfa.org/collections/object/harp-cl%C3%A1irseach-50327

Mytum, H. (2000). *Recording and analysing graveyards*. London: Council for British Archaeology.

Mytum, H. (2004). *Mortuary monuments and burial grounds of the historic period*. New York, NY: Kluwer Academic/Plenum.

Mytum, H. (2006). Popular attitudes to memory, the body, and social identity: The rise of external commemoration in Britain Ireland and New England. *Post-Medieval Archaeology*, 40, 96–110.

Mytum, H. (2017). Mortuary culture. In C. Richardson, T. Hamling, & D. Gaimster (Eds), *The Routledge handbook of material culture in early modern Europe* (pp. 154–167). London/New York, NY: Routledge.

Native Land. (2020). *Native land*. Retrieved from http://native-land.ca/

NPS. (2015). *Historic Jamestowne: Part of Colonial National Historical Park*. Jamestowne, VA: National Park Service. Retrieved from https://www.nps.gov/jame/learn/historyculture/jamestown-churches.htm. Accessed on December 13, 2019.

Pastore, R. (1989). The collapse of the Beothuk world. *Acadiensis: Journal of the History of the Atlantic Region*, 19(1), 52–71. [Electronic document]. Retrieved from https://journals-lib-unb-ca.qe2a-proxy.mun.ca/index.php/Acadiensis/article/view/12292/13136. Accessed on June 6, 2017.

Pearson, H., & Pearson, H. (1913). *Vignettes of Portsmouth: Being representations of divers historic places in old Portsmouth*. Portsmouth/New Hampshire: Helen Pearson and Harold Hotchkiss Bennett. Retrieved from https://archive.org/details/vignettesofports00benn

Perkins, F. H. (1902). *Handbook of Old Burial Hill, Plymouth, Massachusetts: Its history, its famous dead, and its quaint epitaphs*. Plymouth, MA: A.A. Burbank, Pilgrim Bookstore. Retrieved from https://archive.org/details/handbookofoldbur00perki

Pocius, G. L. (1981). Eighteenth- and nineteenth-century Newfoundland gravestones: Self-sufficiency, economic specialization, and the creation of artifacts. *Material Culture Review*, 12(Spring), 1–16.

Pocius, G. L. (1986). The transformation of the traditional Newfoundland cemetery: Institutionalizing the secular dead. *Material Culture Review*, 23(Spring), 25–34.

Pope, P. E. (1993). *Documents relating to Ferryland 1597 to 1726: A textbase, including original transcriptions. Past present – Historic sites and material culture consulting*. Torbay: NFLD.

Powers, N., & Renshaw, L. (2016). The archaeology of post-medieval death and burial. *Post-Medieval Archaeology, 50*(1), 159–177.

Powicke, F. M. (1941). *The reformation in England*. London: Oxford University Press.

Riordan, T. B. (2000). *Dig a grave both wide and deep: An archaeological investigation of mortuary practices in the 17th-century cemetery at St. Mary's City, Maryland*. St. Mary's City Archaeological Series No. 3. St. Mary's City, MD: Historic St. Mary's City.

Riordan, T. B. (2009). "Carry me to Yon Kirk yard": An investigation of changing burial practices in the seventeenth-century cemetery at St. Mary's City, Maryland. *Historical Archaeology, 43*(1), 81–92.

Roads, S. Jr. (1880). *The history and traditions of Marblehead*. Cambridge/Boston, MA: Houghton, Osgood and Company/The Riverside Press. Retrieved from https://archive.org/details/historytradition00road

Rodwell, W. (2012). *The archaeology of Churches*. Gloucestershire: Amberley.

Rugg, J. (2000). Defining the place of burial: What makes a cemetery a cemetery? *Mortality, 5*(3), 259–275.

Rugg, J. (2013a). Choice and constraint in the burial landscape: Re-evaluating twentieth-century commemoration in the English churchyard. *Mortality, 18*(3), 215–234.

Rugg, J. (2013b). *Churchyard and cemetery: Tradition and modernity in rural North Yorkshire*. Manchester: Manchester University Press.

Sachs, A. (2010). America Arcadia: Mount Auburn cemetery and the nineteenth-century landscape tradition. *Environmental Historic, 15*, 206–235.

Sanghra, L. (2012). *Angels and belief in England, 1480–1700: Religious cultures in the early modern world.* London: Routledge.

Sattenspiel, L., & Stoops, M. (2010, May). Gleaning signals about the past from cemetery data. *American Journal of Physical Anthropology, 142*(1), 7–21.

Sayer, D. (2011). Death and the dissenter: Group identity and stylistic simplicity as witnessed in nineteenth-century nonconformist gravestones. *Society for Historical Archaeology, 45*(4), 115–134.

Sexton, J. (2002). The Guilford green: An ever-changing landscape. *Connecticut Trust for Historic Preservation* [Electronic document]. Retrieved from http://www.towngreens.com/DOCUMENTS/tg_guilford_case.pdf. Accessed on December 6, 2016.

Slater, J. A. (1987). *The colonial burying grounds of eastern Connecticut and the men who made them.* Memoirs of the Connecticut Academy of Arts & Sciences. Hamden, CT: Archon Books.

Sloane, D. C. (1991). *The last great necessity: Cemeteries in American history.* Baltimore, MD: Johns Hopkins University Press.

Smith, R. D. (1877). *The history of Guilford, Connecticut.* Albany, NY: J. Munsell. Retrieved from https://archive.org/details/historyofguilfor00smitiala

Souza, J. (2016). The old burial ground on the commons. *Sakonnet Historical* [Electronic document]. Retrieved from http://sakonnethistorical.org/items/show/15. Accessed on December 8, 2016.

Spiwak, A. (2020). *A slator or two: Exploring the 17th-century slate industry at Ferryland*. Master thesis, Department of Archaeology, Memorial University of Newfoundland, St. John's, Newfoundland.

Stanley-Blackwell, L., & Linkletter, M. (2019). Inscribing ethnicity: A preliminary analysis of Gaelic headstone inscriptions in eastern Nova Scotia and Cape Breton. *Genealogy*, 2(3), 241–255.

Stannard, D. E. (1977). *The Puritan way of death: A study in religion, culture, and social change*. New York, NY: Oxford University Press.

Tarlow, S. (1999). *Bereavement and commemoration: An archaeology or mortality*. Oxford: Blackwell.

Tarlow, S. (2016). *The archaeology of death in post-medieval Europe*. Berlin/Boston, MA: De Gruyter.

Thomson, G. (2009). *Inscribed in remembrance: Gravestone lettering: Form, function and recording*. Dublin: Wordwell.

Thorton, K., & Phillips, C. B. (2009). Performing the good death: The medieval Ars Moriendi and contemporary doctors. *Journal of Medical Ethics: Medical Humanities*, 35(2), 94–97.

Trask, D. (1978). *Life how short eternity how long: Gravestone carvings and carvers in Nova Scotia, an illustrated study*. Halifax: The Nova Scotia Museum.

Tuck, J. (1976). *Newfoundland and Labrador prehistory*. Ottawa: National Museum of Man.

Urns for Ashes. (2018). National cremation statistics 1960–2017. *The Cremation Society of Great Britain*. Retrieved from https://www.urnsforashes.co.uk/cremation-statistics/

Winter, M. (2012). Storm unearths very old skeletons in New Haven Park. *USA Today*, October 31. Retrieved from https://www.usatoday.com/story/news/nation/2012/10/31/sandy-skeleton-found-under-new-haven-tree/1672461/

Worpole, K. (2003). *Last landscape: The architecture of the cemetery in the west.* London: Reaktion Books.

Yalom, M. (2008). *The American resting place: Four hundred years of history through our cemeteries and burial grounds.* Boston, MA: Houghton Mifflin.

Yoder, D., & Graves, T. E. (2000). *Hex signs: Pennsylvania Dutch barn symbols and their meaning* (2nd ed.). Mechanicsburg, PA: Stackpole Books.

INDEX

Act of Tolerance, 54
American Resting Place, The (Yalom), 8–9
Anglican, 27
   Anglican/English churchyard model, 88–89
   'King's Chapel', 46–47
Anglican Book of Common Pray (1662), 137
Apotropaic marks, 68
Archaeologists, 1–2
'*Archaeology of American Cemeteries and Gravestones*', The (Baugher and Veit), 16–17
Avalon Peninsula, 136

Baltimore City, 87–88
'Brick Chapel', 87–88
Bristol and London Company, 43
British burial traditions, 19–20
   protestant reformation effects on, 37–43

British colonial period, 32–33
British gravestone in North America, 59–60
British in seventeenth century Newfoundland, 108–112
British Isles, 4–5, 26–27, 32–33
British North America
   17th century burial landscapes in, 77–78
   in early seventeenth century, 43–50
   frequency analysis for comparison between regions, 100
   frequency analysis of seventeenth century settlements, 100
   results of analysis, 99–105
   settlement organization in 17th century, 80–95

seventeenth to eighteenth century British settlements, 84–85
statistical analysis of burial ground organization, 95–99
British settlers, 26–27
British-founded settlements, 26–27
'Britishness' in colonial settlements, 19–21
Burial Act (1880), 44–45
Burial grounds, 3–4, 8–9, 11–14, 24, 53, 79–80
statistical analysis of burial ground organization, 95–99
Burial(s), 1–2
burial/burying ground, 26
cemeteries, 8–9, 24–26
churchyard/graveyard, 24
interments, 3
landscapes, 7–11, 22–24
rites in Britain preceding protestant reformation, 31–37
site at Ferryland, 6–7
space organization, 42–43
terminology, 22–27

Cadaver tombs, 35–36
Carved gravestones, 59–60
Carvers, 14–15
Carvings, 14–15

Catholic epitaphs, 41–42
Catholicism, 132
Catholics, 129–130
Cemeteries, 19–20, 25–26
garden, 25–26
Chantry chapels, 33–34
Chapel Field cemetery, 58–59
'Chapell', 92–93
Christian symbols, 71
Churchyard, 24–25, 54
Cláirseach, 70
'Coffin-less burial', 58–59
Coffins, 51–52, 55–56
styles and accessibility, 57–58
Colonial
burial grounds, 32–33
gravestone carvers, 14–15
Colonialism, 3–4
'Colony of Avalon', 87
British and Irish in seventeenth century Newfoundland, 108–112
evidence of deaths at Ferryland, 112–114
Guilford, Connecticut, 122–127
seventeenth century burials at Ferryland, 114–122
Commemoration, 33–34
Common Burying Ground, 91–92
Communal coffin, 55–56
'Communion tables', 39–40

Index

Conception Bay South, 136–137
Connecticut, 88–90, 102–103
Copp's Hill Burying Ground, 46–47, 91
Copper pins, 55
'Counterreformation ideology', 16–17
Cremation, 36–37
Cupids, 43, 93–95

Daisy wheel. *See* Hexfoil
Death, 1–2, 33–34
  evidence at Ferryland, 112–114
  head, 66–67
'Dig a Grave both Wide and Deep' report, 13–14
Diggers, 44–45
'Dissolution of the Monasteries', 38
Doctrine of calvinism, 38–39

East Coast
  17th-century burial practices and landscapes on, 51
  gravestones in seventeenth-century Atlantic world, 59–65
  seventeenth-century gravestone iconography, 65–76
  below surface, 54–59

Ebola, 130–131
Embalming, 31–32, 36–37
English churchyard model, 98
Enthusiasts, 44–45
European model of 'grave recycling', 131
Excavations, 56–59
  at Ferryland, 107–108, 121
  at Foxtrap, 136–137

Family plots, 86–87
Ferryland, 5–6, 43, 60–61, 109–111
  death evidence at, 112–114
  excavations at, 107–108, 121
  gravestones, 62–63, 65
  pool, 117
  seventeenth century burials at, 114–122
  to St. John's and cupids, 110
Folk traditions, 95
Foxtrap, excavations at, 136–137

Google Earth Pro, 21–22, 97–99
Granary Burying Ground, 91
Grave(s), 116, 135–136
  burial ground, 92–93
  European model of grave recycling, 131
  markers, 14–18
  shafts, 116

Gravestone(s), 14–15, 40, 75–76
  in seventeenth-century Atlantic world, 59–65
  of William Paddy, 64
'*Gravestones of Early New England and the Men who Made Them*' (Forbes), 14
Graveyard, 24–26
  theory, 19–20
Great Awakening, 16–17
Great Migration (1630s), 90–91
Ground penetrating radar (GPR), 116, 119–120
Ground-truthing, 58–59
Guilford, Connecticut, 122–127
Guilford Green, 124–126

Hexafoil. *See* Hexfoil
Hexagonal coffins, 57–58
Hexfoil, 68–74

Iceberg, 6–7
Iconoclasm, 40–41
Iconography, 65–76
Inscribed gravestones, 59–60
Irish
  settlers, 26–27
  in seventeenth century Newfoundland, 108–112
Isabella Stewart Gardner Museum, 91

Jamestown, 43, 81–86
  gravestones, 65
  ledger, 63–64
John Coney stone, 73–74
John Guy's Cupids Plantation, 93–94
JR102C individual, 56–57

King's Chapel Burying Ground, 45–46

Landscape, 1–2, 7–8
  archaeology theory, 53
Lydia Broun stone, 73–74

'Marking grave', 8–9
Massachusetts Bay Company, 43–45, 90–93, 102
'Meeting House Yard', 88–89
Memento mori motifs, 66–67
Menunkatucket, 123
Microsoft Excel, 21–22
Monastic communities, 38
Monumental brasses, 41–42
Monuments, 35
Morbid space, 7–8
Muggletonians, 44–45

Nails, 57–58
New England gravestone art, 14
Newfoundland Company, 5, 20, 43, 51–52, 60–61

Parish coffin, 55–56

'Percy' individual, 56–57
'Pilgrims', 44–45
Plymouth Colony, 90–91
Plymouth plantation, 44–45
Poole Plantation, 113–114
Popham Colony, 92–93
Portable X-ray fluorescence (pXRF), 61–62
Pre-Reformation monuments and gravestones, 35
Preiconography gravestones, 64–65
Protective marks in mortuary context, 68–76
Protestant, 27
Protestant reformation, 129
  on British burial tradition, 37–43
  British North America in early seventeenth century, 43–50
  burial rites in Britain preceding protestant reformation, 31–37
  effects, 31–32
Protestantism, 19–20, 49, 78–79
Purgatory concept, 33–34, 38–39
Puritanism, 16–17, 45–48
Puritans, 15–16, 27, 38–39, 42, 44–45, 129–130
  gravestones, 63–64

Quaker(s), 15–16, 26, 44–45
  gravestones, 63–64

Reform Act (1832), 54
Rhode Island, 90
Romano–British gravestones, 69
Rooms Provincial Museum of Newfoundland and Labrador, 70
Round-end graves, 58–59
Rural cemetery, 25–26
Rural garden cemetery, 25–26

Seekers, 44–45
Settlement
  organization in 17th century, 80–95
  planning, 47–48
Seventeenth century
  burials at Ferryland, 114–122
  settlers, 133
Shrouds, 55
'Six-feet-under' phrase, 58–59
Six-sided cross, 69
Sleeping chamber (*koimeterion*), 25–26
Statistical analysis, 10, 77–78
  of burial ground organization, 95–99
Statistical Package for the Social Sciences (SPSS), 21–22

Thomas Smith stone, 73–74
'Thunder mark', 69–70
Trenches, 116–121

Vandalism theory, 62–63
Virginia Company, 20–21, 43–44
'Virginia', 43, 81–86

Whorl or pinwheel design, 68
Winged skull. *See* Death—head
Witch hex. *See* Hexfoil
Wound shroud, 55

Yorktown, 81–87

Printed and bound by CPI Group (UK) Ltd, Croydon, CR0 4YY

22/11/2023

08193231-0001